Praise for the Second Edition of *The New Taxonomy of Educational Objectives*

"Rich and theory based, incorporating what we have learned about knowledge, thinking, and cognition in the last 50 years. Also quite practical, demonstrating how this new taxonomy can be used as a framework for standards, assessments, and curriculum."

—Carol A. Bartell
Assistant Director, Teachers for a New Era
California State University, Northridge

"Marzano and Kendall provide a critical, theoretically consistent overview of educational objectives with detailed examples of assessment frameworks that bring the 'new' taxonomy to life. The focus on curriculum design that embeds rigorous assessment is a helpful contribution to a new generation of educators challenged to implement content standards for student learning."

—Michelle Collay
Associate Professor
California State University, East Bay

"Educational leaders wishing to infuse greater complexity, rigor, and substance into the curriculum will immerse themselves in *The New Taxonomy of Educational Objectives*. The benefactors will be teachers who will reach beyond their current achievements and students who will develop the intellectual prowess required to master the intricacies, dichotomies, and ambiguities of life in the twenty-first and twenty-second centuries."

—Arthur L. Costa
Professor Emeritus
California State University, Sacramento

"Provides educators with a crisp, new lens to re-examine thinking and learning. Motivation and metacognition, two critical components, are now strategically and meaningfully integrated in a new taxonomy. This revised hierarchy takes us beyond Bloom toward a better understanding of educational theory and practice."

—Virginia Cotsis
Secondary Curriculum Specialist
Ventura County Office of Education, Camarillo, California

"Provides fresh ideas and a set of 'thinking protocols' to help us remember that a primary focus in education must be to develop the mental abilities of our students."

—Lynn Erickson
Curriculum Design Consultant
C & I Consulting, Washington

"A real contribution to the field of education. Provides a well-defined platform for making critical learning skills the basis of skills-based instruction."

—Concha Delgado Gaitan
Author and Independent Researcher
California

"Marzano's Taxonomy skillfully advances the concepts, categories, and conversations related to educational objectives and equips learners and teachers with an interconnected and comprehensive design for processing and expressing thoughts, words, and actions."

—Nancy P. Gallavan
Associate Dean and Professor
College of Education, University of Central Arkansas

"Marzano's Taxonomy will be of immediate and lasting use to curriculum developers, researchers, preparers of teachers and leaders, and practitioners involved in all aspects of standards-based learning. Timely, clearly written, easy to follow, and filled with strong examples and connections to Bloom's Taxonomy."

—Doug Harris
Co-Director
The Center for Curriculum Renewal, Vermont

"Marzano and Kendall haven't simply revised Bloom's Taxonomy. They have forged a thoroughly researched groundwork for numerous educational uses."

—Gregg E. Humphrey
Director of Elementary Education
Middlebury College, Vermont

"Marzano and Kendall provide the necessary ingredients to help fulfill the rhetoric that all kids can learn—and at a high level of thinking! This book informs work on standards at the state and local levels and provides clear examples to assist teachers in their curriculum and assessment design work."

—Bena Kallick
Educational Consultant and Vice President
Performance Pathways, Connecticut

"Marzano and Kendall provide a clear, practical model for educators to follow when developing objectives, assessments, and lessons to improve student achievement. Teachers, teacher leaders, curriculum specialists, and administrators will all find this new taxonomy an essential resource!"

—Ellen Kottler
Lecturer
California State University, Fullerton

"Fully reflects the impressive advancements in the last few decades. Marzano's Taxonomy provides educators with a practical tool to improve the effectiveness of their teaching and their students' learning by helping educators more explicitly frame educational objectives and assessment, use state standards, and design general and thinking skills curricula."

—Dale Lick
Professor
Florida State University

"A pioneering approach to critical and higher-order thinking skills with implications for designing educational objectives, framing curricula design, and implementing national standards and assessments. To prepare elementary and secondary school teachers for teaching a thinking-based curriculum, this book should be part of every undergraduate and graduate teaching program across the country."

—Douglas Llewellyn
Professor of Science Education
St. John Fisher College, New York

"A masterful synthesis, incorporating extensive analysis of state and national content standards with insights from cognitive psychology to produce a more contemporary educational schema. Like a new version of computer software, Marzano's Taxonomy offers a significant upgrade to the classic work of Benjamin Bloom and his colleagues."

—Jay McTighe
Author and Consultant
Jay McTighe and Associates, Maryland

"A clearly practical model that becomes a very powerful tool for educators. The concept sizzles with innovation."

—Carolyn Orange
Professor of Educational Psychology
University of Texas, San Antonio

"This text is astoundingly important. A serious must-read for understanding global issues in developing educational objectives."

—Caroline R. Pryor
Assistant Professor and Wye Fellow
Southern Illinois University, Edwardsville

"Profound in its insights and challenging in its implications, Marzano's Taxonomy will influence teaching, assessment, and accountability in every school. The authors force us to confront the gulf between current standards and testing regimes and the opportunity for sustained learning for which Marzano's Taxonomy will be the framework."

—Douglas Reeves
CEO and Founder
Center for Performance Assessment, Massachusetts

The New
Taxonomy of
Educational
Objectives

Second Edition

Robert J. Marzano
John S. Kendall

The New
Taxonomy of
Educational
Objectives

Second Edition

CORWIN PRESS
A SAGE Publications Company
Thousand Oaks, CA 91320

For information:

Corwin Press
A Sage Publications Company
2455 Teller Road
Thousand Oaks, California 91320
www.corwinpress.com

Sage Publications Ltd.
1 Oliver's Yard
55 City Road
London EC1Y 1SP
United Kingdom

Sage Publications India Pvt. Ltd.
B-42, Panchsheel Enclave
Post Box 4109
New Delhi 110 017 India

Printed in the United States of America

Library of Congress Cataloging-in-Publication Data

Marzano, Robert J.
The new taxonomy of educational objectives / Robert J. Marzano, John S. Kendall.—2nd ed.
      p. cm.
Includes bibliographical references and index.
ISBN 1-4129-3628-4 or 978-1-4129-3628-6 (cloth)—
ISBN 1-4129-3629-2 or 978-1-4129-3629-3 (pbk.)
   1. Education—Aims and objectives. I. Kendall, John S. II. Title.
LB17.M394 2007
370.1—dc22   2006020923

This book is printed on acid-free paper.

11 12 13 14 15 10 9 8 7 6 5 4 3

Acquisitions Editor:	Rachel Livsey
Editorial Assistant:	Phyllis Cappello
Production Editor:	Laureen A. Shea
Copy Editor:	Marilyn Power Scott
Typesetter:	C&M Digitals (P) Ltd.
Proofreader:	Theresa Kay
Indexer:	Kathy Paparchontis
Cover Designer:	Monique Hahn

Contents

Preface

The *Taxonomy of Educational Objectives* (Bloom, Engelhart, Furst, Hill, & Krathwohl, 1956) was published a half century ago. Since that time a number of attempts have been made to revise Bloom's Taxonomy so that it incorporates modern advances in the understanding of human thought and the structure of knowledge. This volume represents our update of Bloom's Taxonomy, and we argue that as a practical tool for educators it is superior to all other attempts to date. In fact, this volume is the progeny of an earlier version titled *Designing a New Taxonomy of Educational Objectives* published in 2001 (Marzano, 2001). As the title of that volume indicates, it was presented as a "work in progress"—an initial step in the development of a new taxonomy: "Though it has used the best available information regarding the nature of knowledge and the manner in which the human mind processes information, the New Taxonomy as described here will surely be revised over time" (p. 130). Since its publication, that work has been used and field tested in a wide variety of venues with a wide variety of audiences. This work, *The New Taxonomy of Educational Objectives,* is the revision of the 2001 publication. As the title indicates, it is presented as a "work completed."

The New Taxonomy as described in this book has many similarities with the framework presented in 2001. However, it has a number of noteworthy departures. One is that it addresses its differences with and advantages over the Anderson et al. (2001) revision of Bloom's Taxonomy as a practical tool for educators. Another is that it more explicitly explains specific applications of the New Taxonomy: (1) as a framework for designing and classifying educational objectives, (2) as a framework for designing assessments, (3) as a tool for making state standards more useful to educators, (4) as a structure for designing curriculum, and (5) as the basis for a thinking skills curriculum. It is our hope that educators use the New Taxonomy to enhance the effectiveness of their teaching and deepen the learning of their students.

ACKNOWLEDGMENTS

The contributions of the following reviewers are gratefully acknowledged:

Jay McTighe
Education Writer and Consultant
McTighe and Associates, Consulting
Columbia, MD

Kathy Grover
Assistant Superintendent for Curriculum and Instruction
Clever R-V Public Schools
Clever, MO

Virginia Cotsis
Secondary Curriculum Specialist
Educational Services Division
Curriculum and Instruction
Ventura County Office of Education
Camarillo, CA

Lorin W. Anderson
Carolina Distinguished Professor Emeritus
University of South Carolina
Columbia, SC

Douglas Harris
Co-Director
The Center for Curriculum Renewal
Sarasota, FL

Roberta Richin
Author and Co-Founder
"Connecting Character to Conduct" Consultants
Stony Brook, NY

About the Authors

Dr. Robert J. Marzano is Senior Scholar at Mid-continent Research for Education and Learning (McREL) in Aurora, Colorado, Associate Professor at Cardinal Stritch University in Milwaukee, Wisconsin, and President of Marzano & Associates in Centennial, Colorado. He is the author of 25 books, 150 articles and chapters in books, and 100 sets of curriculum materials for teachers and students in Grades K–12. His works include *What Works in Schools: Translating Research Into Action, School Leadership That Works, Building Background Knowledge for Academic Achievement, Classroom Management That Works, Classroom Instruction That Works, Classroom Assessment and Grading That Work,* and *A Different Kind of Classroom: Teaching With Dimensions of Learning.*

During his 35 years in public education, Marzano has worked in every state multiple times as well as in a host of countries in Europe and Asia. The central theme in his work has been translating research and theory into practical programs and tools for K–12 teachers and administrators.

John S. Kendall is a Senior Director in research at McREL. There he directs a technical assistance unit that develops and provides standards-related services for schools, districts, states, and other organizations. Clients have included Achieve, Inc., The College Board, and NASA's Jet Propulsion Lab. He has been with McREL 17 years as Research Assistant, Program Associate, and Senior Director.

An internationally recognized expert in the development and improvement of standards for education, Kendall has consulted for more than 50 school districts and 14 state departments of education as well as education agencies in the U.S. territories and abroad. Senior author of *Content Knowledge: A Compendium of Standards and Benchmarks for K–12 Education,* he has authored or coauthored six books and more than 30 monographs, technical studies, and articles published by *American School Board Journal,* Association for Supervision and Curriculum Development, and National Association of School Boards, among others. He received his undergraduate and master's degrees from the University of Colorado at Boulder.

Kendall's current research and technical assistance efforts include working with clients to establish performance standards for the classroom, developing standards for principals, and identifying the knowledge and skills that help students learn.

CHAPTER ONE

The Need for a Revision of Bloom's Taxonomy

I n 1956, a small, somewhat technical volume was published under the title, *Taxonomy of Educational Objectives, The Classification of Educational Goals, Handbook I: Cognitive Domain* (Bloom et al., 1956). In the 50-plus years since its publication, "Bloom's Taxonomy," as it is frequently referred to in deference to Benjamin Bloom, the work's editor, has been used by educators in virtually every subject area at virtually every grade level. The expressed purpose of the taxonomy was to develop a codification system whereby educators could design learning objectives that have a hierarchical organization.

> You are reading about an attempt to build a taxonomy of educational objectives. It is intended to provide for classification of the goals of our educational system. It is expected to be of general help to all teachers, administrators, professional specialists, and research workers who deal with curricular and evaluation problems. (p. 1)

That Bloom's Taxonomy is still used after some 50 years is a testament to its contribution to education and psychology. Indeed, the 93rd yearbook of the National Society for the Study of Education (NSSE), titled *Bloom's Taxonomy: A Forty-Year Retrospective*, documents the impact of the work:

> Arguably, one of the most influential educational monographs of the past half century is the *Taxonomy of Educational Objectives, The Classification of Educational Goals, Handbook I: Cognitive Domain*. Nearly forty years after its publication in 1956 the volume remains a standard reference for discussions of testing and evaluation, curriculum development, and teaching and teacher education. A search of the most recent *Social*

Science Citation Index (1992) revealed more than 150 citations to the *Handbook.* At a recent meeting of approximately 200 administrators and teachers, the senior editor of this volume asked for a show of hands in response to the question, "How many of you have heard of Bloom's Taxonomy?" Virtually every hand in the audience was raised. Few education publications have enjoyed such overwhelming recognition for so long. (Anderson & Sosniak, 1994, p. vii)

Those interested in a thorough discussion of the many uses and analyses of Bloom's Taxonomy should consult the 1994 NSSE yearbook. However, a brief synopsis is useful here.

A Brief History of the Use of Bloom's Taxonomy

A scrutiny of the past 50-plus years in education indicates that Bloom's Taxonomy has had a significant, albeit uneven, influence on educational theory and practice. According to Peter Airasian (1994), the taxonomy fitted nicely into the instructional objectives movement that attained national prominence after the publication of Robert Mager's (1962) *Preparing Instructional Objectives.* Mager's book was explicitly designed to help those intending to develop a methodology of programmed instruction and was based on the premise that cognitive tasks could be ordered hierarchically. Airasian (1994) notes that "one might think, given this affinity, that the taxonomy would have been an influential tool in the development of programmed instructional sequences. In one sense it was" (p. 87). As Edgar Dale (1967) explains, Bloom's Taxonomy became the structure around which many initial efforts at programmed instruction were organized. However, Airasian (1994) argues that Bloom's Taxonomy was ultimately replaced by Gagne's (1977) framework as the conceptual organizer for programmed instruction. Although Gagne's framework was less hierarchical than Bloom's Taxonomy, it was more easily translated into instructional practice.

Whereas Bloom's Taxonomy had a minimal influence on curriculum, it had a strong effect on evaluation. By 1970, Ralph Tyler's model of evaluation design was fairly well established. Specifically, Tyler presented an objectives-based view of evaluation in which a program or an instructional intervention was evaluated on the extent to which it had accomplished its explicit goals (for a discussion of Tyler's model, see Madaus & Stufflebeam, 1989). The more precisely goals were stated, the more precisely a program could be evaluated. Bloom's Taxonomy proved to be a powerful tool for objectives-based evaluation in that it allowed for a level of detail in stating goals that had not previously been readily attained.

Bloom's Taxonomy also proved to be a valuable tool for those who ascribed to the model of evaluation known as the "planning, programming, budgeting system" (PPBS). Initially used in the Pentagon, PPBS followed Tyler's tenets of objectives-based evaluation in that it was predicated on first identifying the intended outcomes of a program, then measuring the extent to which these outcomes had been achieved at the program's conclusion. This system became popular in education when it was adopted as the primary tool for evaluating the effectiveness of the 1965 Elementary and Secondary Education Act (ESEA), which was a direct consequence of President Lyndon Johnson's War on Poverty. Under ESEA, Title I funds were allocated to provide additional educational services to lower-achieving students in schools having large proportions of children from low-income backgrounds. Airasian (1994) explains that "for the first time in history substantial amounts of federal aid, more than a billion dollars a year at its inception, were funneled into local school districts to meet the educational needs of disadvantaged children" (p. 89). Given the scale of the financial aid available to schools under Title I, some politicians demanded reporting requirements that would ensure the monies were being used appropriately. Eventually, PPBS became the preferred Title I assessment vehicle and Bloom's Taxonomy the preferred system for articulating program objectives.

The 1970s also marked the beginning of statewide testing. Indeed, in 1960 only one state had a mandated statewide test; by 1985, 32 states had mandated tests. Virtually every state test was designed to provide information about student achievement on specific topics within specific subject areas, and virtually every state test made use of Bloom's Taxonomy, at least to some extent, to define various levels of skill. By the mid-1970s, state tests began to take a minimum-competency approach. As Airasian (1987) explained, minimum-competency tests were different from the more general forms of tests in at least three ways: (1) They were mandated for all schools and virtually all students within a state in which their predecessors could be administered to representative samples of students; (2) the mandate took away much, if not all, of individual districts' discretion in terms of test selection, administration, scoring, and interpretation; and (3) the tests had built-in sanctions if specific levels of performance were not met. Again, Bloom's Taxonomy was widely used as the model for designing items that measure low-level or basic skills versus so-called higher-level skills.

The 1980s saw the beginning of an emphasis on teaching higher levels of thinking. It was this movement, along with research on the validity of Bloom's Taxonomy (reviewed in a subsequent section), that raised awareness as to the need to revise it. A barrage of books, articles, and reports appeared, supporting the need for instruction in thinking and reasoning skills. For example, such prominent organizations as the Education Commission of the States (1982) and the College Entrance Examination Board (1983) highlighted the need to teach thinking. High-impact reports, such as *A Nation at Risk* (National Commission, 1983), pointed to deficiencies in higher-level thinking as a major weakness in American education. Widely read journals, such as *Educational Leadership* and *Review of Educational Research,* devoted entire volumes to the topic (e.g., see Brandt, 1986, and Glasman & Pellegrino, 1984, respectively). Many of these publications cited evidence of students' inability to answer higher-level questions and apply their knowledge.

In May 1984, the Association for Supervision and Curriculum Development (ASCD) called a meeting at the Wingspread Conference Center in Racine, Wisconsin, to consider possible solutions to the problem of students' poor performance on tasks that demand higher-level thinking. One of the suggestions from the conference was that Bloom's Taxonomy should be updated to include current research and theory on the nature of knowledge and the nature of cognition (for a discussion of that conference, see Marzano, Brandt, et al., 1988). As a direct result of that conference, the Association Collaborative for Teaching Thinking was formed. Twenty-eight organizations were official participants in the collaborative, including

American Association of School Administrators

American Association of School Librarians

American Educational Research Association

American Federation of Teachers

Association for Supervision and Curriculum Development

Council of Chief State School Officers

Home Economics Education Association

International Reading Association

Music Educators National Conference

National Alliance of Black School Educators

National Art Education Association

National Association of Elementary School Principals

National Association of Secondary School Principals

National Council for the Social Studies

National Council of Teachers of English

National Council of Teachers of Mathematics

National Education Association

National Middle School Association

National School Boards Association

National Science Teachers Association

Unfortunately, the collaborative never produced a revision of Bloom's Taxonomy.

BLOOM'S TAXONOMY: A SUMMARY

Given that this work is designed to update Bloom's Taxonomy, it is useful to briefly review it. In its most general form, Bloom's Taxonomy outlines six levels of cognitive processes:

1.00 Knowledge

2.00 Comprehension

3.00 Application

4.00 Analysis

5.00 Synthesis

6.00 Evaluation

Each level is designed to possess defining characteristics.

1.00 Knowledge

The *knowledge* level is operationally defined as information retrieval: "Knowledge as defined here includes those behaviors and test situations which emphasize the remembering, either by recognition or recall, of ideas, materials or phenomena" (Bloom et al., 1956, p. 62). A close examination of this first category shows that Bloom articulates specific types of knowledge, which include the following categories and subcategories:

1.10   Specifics
     1.11 Terminology
     1.12 Facts

1.20   Ways and means of dealing with specifics
     1.21 Conventions
     1.22 Trends and sequences
     1.23 Classification and categories
     1.24 Criteria
     1.25 Methodology

Bloom's category of knowledge, then, mixes the cognitive process of retrieval with the various types of knowledge that are retrieved.

2.00 Comprehension

Comprehension represents the largest class of intellectual skills and abilities. The central feature of the act of comprehension is taking in new information via some form of communication ("when students are confronted with a communication, they are expected to know what is being communicated and to be able to make some use of the materials or ideas contained in it" [p. 89]). The taxonomy does not limit communication to the presentation of information in linguistic (verbal or written) form. Rather, information can be presented symbolically or experientially. Thus a student attempting to understand the ideas underlying a demonstration would be involved in the act of comprehension.

Three forms of comprehension are described in the taxonomy: translation, interpretation, and extrapolation. *Translation* involves encoding incoming information into some form other than that in which it was received. For example, students would be engaged in translation if they summarized in their own words the information contained in a film on the formation of a tornado. Whereas translation involves the identification of the literal structure underlying the incoming information, *interpretation* "may require a reordering of ideas into a new configuration in the mind" (p. 90). Finally, *extrapolation* goes beyond the literal level of comprehension. It involves inferences and predictions based on literal information in the communication and principles and generalizations already possessed by the learner (p. 90).

3.00 Application

The third category of cognitive skills, *application,* is probably the least-well-defined in Bloom's Taxonomy. It is described in relationship to a specific type of knowledge—abstractions—and is defined primarily in terms of how it compares with other levels of the taxonomy. To illustrate, Bloom notes that the comprehension of an abstraction requires students to know the abstraction well enough that they can

> correctly demonstrate its use when specifically asked to do so. "Application," however, requires a step beyond this. Given a problem new to the student, he will apply the appropriate abstraction without having to be prompted as to which abstraction is correct or without having to be shown how to use it in that situation. (p. 120)

Bloom further explains that an abstraction understood at the level of comprehension can be used only when the conditions for its use are specified. However, the application of an abstraction is demonstrated when one correctly uses the abstraction in a situation in which no mode of solution is specified.

4.00 Analysis

Just as *application* is defined in terms of a subordinate category of Bloom's Taxonomy, *analysis* is defined in terms of application and comprehension. Bloom notes that,

> In *comprehension,* the emphasis is on the grasp of the meaning and intent of the material. In *application* it is on remembering and bringing to bear upon given material the appropriate generalizations or principles. *Analysis* emphasizes the detection of relationships of the parts and of the way they are organized. (p. 144)

Analysis is divided into three subcategories: the identification or classification of (1) elements, (2) relationships among elements, and (3) organizational principles that govern elements (p. 145).

Admittedly, this category overlaps with the categories of comprehension and evaluation: "No entirely clear lines can be drawn between analysis and comprehension at one end or between analysis and evaluation at the other" (p. 144).

5.00 Synthesis

Synthesis primarily involves the generation of new knowledge structures.

> Synthesis is defined here as putting together elements and parts as to form a whole. This is a process of working with elements, parts, etc., and combining them in such a way as to constitute a pattern or structure not clearly there before. Generally, this would involve a recombination of parts of previous experiences with new material, reconstructed into a new and more or less well-integrated whole. (p. 162)

Bloom explains that this category of cognition most clearly calls for creative behavior on the part of the student because it involves newly constructed and oftentimes unique products. Three specific categories of products are defined: (1) unique communications, (2) a plan or set of operations, and (3) a set of abstract relationships.

Again, Bloom acknowledges many similarities between this category and the previous categories: "Comprehension, application, and analysis also involve the putting together of elements and the construction of meanings, but these tend to be more partial and less compatible than synthesis in the magnitude of the task" (p. 162).

6.00 Evaluation

Evaluation involves making judgments about the value of knowledge. According to Bloom, it involves

> the use of criteria as well as standards for appraising the extent to which particulars are accurate, effective, economical, or satisfying. The judgments may be either quantitative or qualitative and the criteria may be either those determined by the student or those which are given to him. (p. 185)

Two forms of criteria or evidence are noted within this category: internal and external. By definition, *evaluation* is a form of decision making, done at a very conscious and thoughtful level, as opposed to decisions that are made quickly without much conscious thought. Bloom refers to the latter as "opinions," as opposed to "judgments," which, by definition, involve evaluation.

PROBLEMS WITH BLOOM'S TAXONOMY

As influential as Bloom's Taxonomy has been on educational practice, it has experienced some severe criticisms (for a review, see Kreitzer & Madaus, 1994). One of the most common criticisms was that the taxonomy oversimplified the nature of thought and its relationship to learning (Furst, 1994). The taxonomy certainly expanded the conception of learning from a simple, unidimensional, behaviorist model to one that was multidimensional and more constructivist in nature. However, it assumed a rather simple construct of difficulty as the characteristic separating one level from another: Superordinate levels involved more difficult cognitive processes than did subordinate levels. The research conducted on Bloom's Taxonomy simply did not support this structure. For example, educators who were trained in the structure of Bloom's Taxonomy were consistently unable to recognize questions at higher levels as more difficult than questions at lower levels of the taxonomy (see Fairbrother, 1975; Poole, 1972; Stanley & Bolton, 1957).

The problems with Bloom's Taxonomy were indirectly acknowledged by its authors. This is evidenced in their discussion of analysis: "It is probably more defensible educationally to consider analysis as an aid to fuller comprehension (a lower class level) or as a prelude to an evaluation of the material" (p. 144). The authors also acknowledged problems with the taxonomy's structure in their discussion of evaluation:

> Although evaluation is placed last in the cognitive domain because it is regarded as requiring to some extent all the other categories of behavior, it is not necessarily the last step in thinking or problem solving. It is quite possible that the evaluation process will in some cases be the prelude to the acquisition of new knowledge, a new attempt at comprehension or application, or a new analysis and synthesis. (p. 185)

In summary, the hierarchical structure of Bloom's Taxonomy simply did not hold together well from logical or empirical perspectives. As Rohwer and Sloane (1994) note, "The structure claimed for the hierarchy, then, *resembles* a hierarchy" (p. 47).

OTHER TAXONOMIES

Since the publication of Bloom's Taxonomy, others have attempted to update and improve on that initial effort. Many of these revisions have been reviewed by Moseley (n.d.) and by de Kock, Sleegers, and Voeten (2004). Depending on what one counts as an update or revision, over 20 can be identified. Of these, the effort most closely associated with Bloom's original work is that undertaken by Anderson et al. (2001). The ties to Bloom's work are many. Indeed, the title of Anderson et al.'s effort makes an explicit connection—*A Taxonomy for Learning, Teaching, and Assessing: A Revision of Bloom's Taxonomy of Educational Objectives*—not to mention the fact that one of the authors—David Krathwohl—was a coauthor of Bloom's original taxonomy. According to Anderson et al., the revision was needed to update the framework in terms of the advances in cognitive psychology since its imprint and to use more "common language" (p. xxii) while articulating more "realistic examples" (p. xxii).

Anderson et al.'s (2001) taxonomy involves two basic dimensions. The first is referred to as the knowledge domain and involves four types of knowledge: factual, conceptual, procedural, and metacognitive. *Factual knowledge* involves "basic elements students must know to be acquainted with a discipline or solve a problem in it" (p. 29). *Conceptual knowledge* involves "the interrelationships among the basic elements within a larger structure that enable them to function together" (p. 29). *Procedural knowledge* involves "how to do something, methods of inquiry, and criteria for using skills, algorithms, techniques, and methods" (p. 29). *Metacognitive* knowledge involves "knowledge of cognition in general as well as awareness and knowledge of one's own cognition" (p. 29).

The second dimension is referred to as the cognitive process domain and involves six types of thinking. *Remembering* involves retrieving "relevant knowledge from long-term memory" (Anderson et al., 2001, p. 31). *Understanding* involves constructing "meaning from instructional messages, including oral, written, and graphic communication." *Applying* involves carrying out or using "a procedure in a given situation." *Analyzing* involves breaking material into constituent parts and determining "how parts relate to one another and to an overall structure or purpose." *Evaluating* involves making "judgments based on criteria and standards." *Creating* involves putting "elements together to form a coherent or functional whole" and reorganizing "elements into a new pattern or structure" (p. 31).

With the elements of both dimensions defined, educational objectives could be classified. To illustrate, Anderson et al. (2001) provide the example of an objective a teacher might establish in a science class: "The student will learn to apply the reduce-reuse-recycle approach to conservation" (p. 32). Since it involves knowledge about "doing something," this objective is classified as procedural along the knowledge dimension. Since the objective involves "carrying out" something, it is classified as application along the cognitive process dimension.

Certainly, the Anderson et al. (2001) effort added significantly to Bloom's original work. In addition, as the ensuing chapter will demonstrate, it has a great deal of similarity with the model we present in this book. However, as the discussion will demonstrate, the New Taxonomy presented here does not suffer from the same pitfalls as Bloom's Taxonomy and its progeny and is arguably friendlier to teachers in terms of its translation to classroom practice.

THE THEORETICAL BASIS FOR A NEW TAXONOMY

As mentioned, one of the problems in the approach taken by Bloom and his colleagues (and that of virtually every other revision or adaptation of Bloom's work) is that it attempted to use degrees of difficulty as the basis of the differences between levels of the taxonomy. Evaluation activities were assumed to be more difficult than activities that involved syntheses, which were assumed to be more difficult than activities involving analysis, and so on. Ultimately, any attempt to design a taxonomy based on difficulty of mental processing is doomed to failure, because of the well-established principle in psychology that even the most complex of processes can be learned at the level at which it is performed with little or no conscious effort (for discussions, see Anderson, 1983, 1990b, 1995; LaBerge, 1995; LaBerge & Samuels, 1974). The difficulty of a mental process is a function of at least two factors—the inherent complexity of the process in terms of steps involved and the level of familiarity one has with the process. The complexity of a mental process is invariant—the number of steps and their relationship do not change. However, familiarity with a process will change over time. The more familiar one is with a process, the more quickly one executes it, and the easier it becomes. To use an obvious example, the process of driving an automobile in rush-hour freeway traffic is very complex in terms of the number of inter-acting and complementary processes that are involved, each with a vast array of component parts. Yet most seasoned drivers would not consider the task difficult and frequently execute it while engaged in other unrelated tasks, such as talking on a cell phone, listening to the radio, and so on.

Although mental processes cannot be ordered hierarchically in terms of difficulty, they can be ordered in terms of control: Some processes exercise control over the operation of other processes. The model used to develop the New Taxonomy as described in this book is presented in Figure 1.1.

Figure 1.1   Model of Behavior

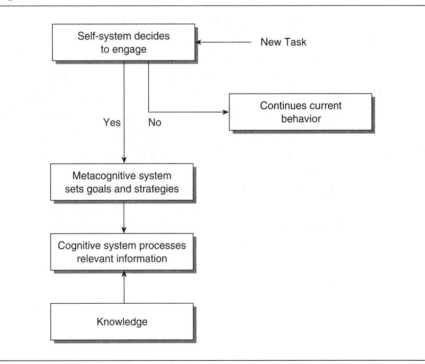

The model depicted in Figure 1.1 not only describes how human beings decide whether to engage in a new task at some point in time, but it also explains how information is processed once a decision to engage has been made. The model presents three mental systems: the self-system, the metacognitive system, and the cognitive system. The fourth component of the model is knowledge.

In this model, a *new task* is defined as an opportunity to change whatever one is doing or attending to at a particular time. For example, assume that a student is in a science class, daydreaming about an upcoming social activity after school, and energy and attention are focused on the social activity. However, if the teacher asked the student to pay attention to some new information that was being presented about science, he or she would be confronted with a decision regarding a new task. The decision made and the subsequent actions would be determined by the interaction of the student's self-, the metacognitive and cognitive systems, as well as his or her knowledge. Specifically, the self-system is engaged first, then the metacognitive system, and finally the cognitive system. All three systems use the student's store of knowledge.

THE THREE SYSTEMS AND KNOWLEDGE

The self-system contains a network of interrelated beliefs and goals (Csikszentmihalyi, 1990; Harter, 1980; Markus & Ruvulo, 1990) that are used to make judgments about the advisability of engaging in a new task. The self-system is also a prime determiner in the motivation one brings to a task (Garcia & Pintrich, 1991, 1993, 1995; Pintrich & Garcia, 1992). If a task is judged important, if the probability of success is high, and positive affect is generated or associated with the task, the individual will be motivated to engage in the new task (Ajzen, 1985; Ajzen & Fishbein, 1977, 1980; Ajzen & Madden, 1986). If the new task is evaluated as having low relevance or low probability of success and has an associated negative affect, motivation to engage in the task is low. To be highly motivated to attend to the new science information, then, the student would have to perceive the information as more important than the social event, believe the information can be comprehended, and have no strong negative emotions associated with it.

If a new task is selected, the metacognitive system is engaged. One of the initial jobs of the metacognitive system is to set goals relative to the new task (Schank & Abelson, 1977). This system is also responsible for designing strategies for accomplishing a given goal once it has been set (Sternberg, 1977, 1984a, 1984b, 1986a, 1986b). In terms of the student in the science class, the metacognitive system would be responsible for setting learning goals relative to the new information and designing strategies to accomplish those goals. The metacognitive system, once engaged, is continually interacting with the cognitive system.

The cognitive system is responsible for the effective processing of the information that is essential to the completion of a task. It is responsible for analytic operations, such as making inference, comparing, classifying, and the like. For example, as our example student listens to the new information, he or she would undoubtedly have to make inferences about it, compare it with what he or she already knows, and so on.

Finally, relative to any new task, success is highly dependent on the amount of knowledge an individual has about that task (Anderson, 1995; Lindsay & Norman, 1977). For example, the extent to which the science student achieves the learning goals would to a great extent depend on prior knowledge about the science topic.

THE NEW TAXONOMY IN BRIEF

The foregoing description underpins the design of the New Taxonomy as depicted in Figure 1.2.

Figure 1.2   The New Taxonomy

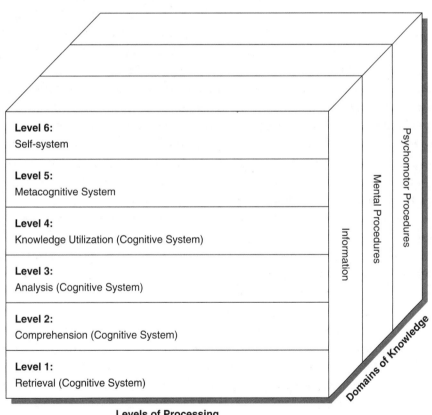

Level 6:
Self-system

Level 5:
Metacognitive System

Level 4:
Knowledge Utilization (Cognitive System)

Level 3:
Analysis (Cognitive System)

Level 2:
Comprehension (Cognitive System)

Level 1:
Retrieval (Cognitive System)

Information   Mental Procedures   Psychomotor Procedures

Domains of Knowledge

Levels of Processing

Here is a brief introduction to the New Taxonomy. The rows on the left-hand side of Figure 1.2 depict the three systems of thought and, in the case of the cognitive system, four subcomponents of that system. The columns depicted on the right-hand side depict three different types or domains of knowledge: information, mental procedures, and psychomotor procedures. The example involving the science student addressed the domain of information, specifically information about science. Had the teacher been a writing teacher wishing to engage the student in practice regarding a specific editing technique, let's say, the example would have addressed the domain of mental procedures. Had the teacher been a physical education teacher wishing to engage the student in a stretching activity, the example would have addressed the domain of psychomotor procedures.

In effect, the New Taxonomy is a two-dimensional model with six categories of mental processes represented by one dimension and three domains of knowledge represented by the other dimension. Educational objectives can be easily classified within these two dimensions. To illustrate, reconsider the objective used by Anderson et al. (2001) to exemplify how their taxonomy can be used to classify educational objectives: "The student will learn to apply the reduce-reuse-recycle approach to conservation" (p. 32). Within the New Taxonomy this objective would be classified as an analysis activity within the cognitive processing dimension, and it would be classified as information within the types of knowledge dimension. This classification is quite different from that obtained using the Anderson et al. taxonomy, where it was classified as application within the cognitive process dimension and as procedural knowledge within the types of knowledge dimension. As we shall see in the next section, this difference is an important one in terms of the utility and interpretation of the two newer taxonomies.

In Chapters 2, 3, and 4, we describe the research and theory underlying the various components of the New Taxonomy and how it provides a context or framework for understanding the relationships between mental processes and types of knowledge. In Chapters 5 and 6 we explain how the New Taxonomy can be used in a variety of ways in educational settings. The most obvious use is as a vehicle for designing and classifying educational objectives. The foregoing examples focused on classifying an educational objective. A desired outcome was articulated by a teacher, and the New Taxonomy was used to determine the type of knowledge involved and the mental process applied to that knowledge. Classifying objectives is by nature a post hoc activity. The New Taxonomy can also be used to generate objectives; using the New Taxonomy can ensure that specific types of knowledge are addressed and processed in specific ways.

A second use of the New Taxonomy is as a framework for designing assessments. In Chapter 5 a case will be made that assessments are the logical consequence of well-articulated objectives. That is, an objective establishes a goal, and an assessment helps determine progress toward that goal. Different types of objectives demand different types of assessments. Therefore, the New Taxonomy provides a framework for generating and understanding classroom assessments.

A third use of the New Taxonomy is as a framework for redesigning state and district-level standards to render them more interpretable and useful for students. It is no exaggeration to say that since its inception, the standards movement has permeated K–12 education in the United States. Robert Glaser and Robert Linn (1993) explain:

> In the recounting of our nation's drive toward educational reform, the last decade of this century will undoubtedly be identified as the time when a concentrated press for national educational standards emerged. The press for standards was evidenced by the efforts of federal and state legislators, presidential and gubernatorial candidates, teachers and subject-matter specialists, councils, governmental agencies, and private foundations. (p. xiii)

Glaser and Linn (1993) made their comments at the end of the twentieth century. There is no indication that the standards movement has lost any momentum at the beginning of the twenty-first century. As powerful as the standards movement has been in the United States, it has probably generated as many problems as it has solutions. One of the most glaring is that standards documents are not easily translated into classroom practice. To remedy this, a number of researchers and theorists have called for the revision of standards documents (Ainsworth, 2003a, 2003b; Reeves, 2002). In particular, Kendall (2000) has demonstrated that rewriting standards documents can make them useful tools for classroom teachers. As will be demonstrated in Chapter 5, the New Taxonomy can be used as a framework for recasting state standards documents.

A fourth use for the New Taxonomy is as a framework for curriculum design. The various levels of the New Taxonomy can be thought of as various types of tasks that form the basis of curriculum design. Different types of tasks serve different ends. Knowledge utilization tasks require students to apply knowledge; analysis tasks require students to examine knowledge from different perspectives. In effect, how a teacher arranges and sequences tasks constitutes the curriculum for a class.

A fifth use of the New Taxonomy is as a framework for a thinking skills curriculum. In her book, *Education and Learning to Think,* Resnick (1987) chronicled the need to design and implement a curriculum of mental skills or "thinking skills." She warned that such a curriculum should not be thought of as "higher order," to be addressed only after students have mastered the basics of the knowledge domains via drill and practice. Higher-order curricula are commonly reserved for those students deemed to exhibit exceptional ability. Rather, such a thinking skills curriculum should be embedded in the traditional subject areas at the earliest possible grade levels: "Indeed, research suggests that failure to cultivate aspects of thinking . . . may be the source of major learning difficulties in the elementary school" (p. 8). To this end the New Taxonomy can form the basis of explicit thinking skills and processes that might be taught in the context of traditional subject matter.

In Chapters 5 and 6, each of these uses will be discussed in more detail.

The New Taxonomy, Bloom's Taxonomy, and the Anderson et al. Revision

How then does the model depicted in Figure 1.1 (and its translation to a taxonomy in Figure 1.2) improve on Bloom's efforts? It does so in at least two ways. First, it presents a model or a *theory* of human thought as opposed to a *framework*. Technically, models and theories are systems that allow one to predict phenomena; frameworks are loosely organized sets of principles that describe characteristics of a given phenomenon but do not necessarily allow for the prediction of phenomena. (For a discussion of models, theories, and frameworks, see Anderson, 1990a.) By definition, Bloom's Taxonomy is a framework in that it describes six general categories of information processing. They are certainly useful categories in helping educators understand the multifaceted nature of learning. Indeed, in his 1977 edition of *Conditions of Learning,* Robert Gagne commented on the ingenious contributions of the authors of the taxonomy to an understanding of the various categories of learning. However, Bloom's Taxonomy was not designed to predict specific behaviors (Rohwer & Sloane, 1994) and is, therefore, not a model or theory. The depiction in Figure 1.1 allows for the prediction of specific behaviors within specific situations. For example, given an understanding of an individual's beliefs within the self-system, one can predict the attention that will be paid to a given task and the motivation that will be displayed.

Second (and more important relative to the discussion), the theory presented here improves on Bloom's effort in that it allows for the design of a hierarchical system of human thought from the perspective of two criteria: (1) flow of information and (2) level of consciousness. Here we briefly consider the criterion of flow of information. The criterion of level of consciousness is discussed at the end of Chapter 3, where the details of the New Taxonomy are articulated.

In terms of flow of information, processing always starts with the self-system, proceeds to the metacognitive system, then to the cognitive system, and finally to the knowledge domains. In addition, the status of the various factors within one system affects the status of the various factors within lower systems. For example, if the self-system contains no beliefs that would render a given task important, the individual will either not engage in the task or engage with low motivation. If the task is deemed important but a clear goal is not established by the metacognitive system, execution of the task will break down. If clear goals have been established and effectively monitored but the information-processing functions within the cognitive system do not operate effectively, the task will not be carried out. The three systems, then, represent a true hierarchy in terms of flow of processing.

Given its link with Bloom's Taxonomy, we should also contrast the Anderson et al. (2001) model with the New Taxonomy. To a great extent, it has the same strengths and weaknesses as Bloom's Taxonomy. This is because it was designed (at least in part) as a revision intended to focus the attention of modern-day educators on the original work: "First, there is a need to refocus educators' attention on the original Handbook, not only as a historical document but as one that in many respects was 'ahead of its time'" (p. xxi). Given this well-intended tie to Bloom's Taxonomy, it suffers from the same inherent weakness of that work—the tacit assumption that its levels are ordered hierarchically in terms of difficulty. As Anderson et al. note, "The continuum underlying the cognitive process dimension is assumed to be cognitive complexity; that is *Understand* is believed to be more cognitively complex than *Remember, Apply* is believed to be more cognitively complex than *Understand,* and so on" (p. 5).

Even though the Anderson et al. (2001) taxonomy was designed as a revision of Bloom's Taxonomy, it has some remarkable similarities with the New Taxonomy. Most noteworthy, the two dimensions employed by the Anderson taxonomy are quite similar to the two dimensions employed in the New Taxonomy. The Anderson taxonomy has a knowledge dimension and a cognitive process dimension. The New Taxonomy has a domain of knowledge dimension and a levels-of-processing dimension. At face value both taxonomies classify educational tasks by considering the type of knowledge that is the focus of instruction and the type of mental processing the task imposes on that knowledge. Both taxonomies, then, employ the suggestions of Ralph Tyler (1949b) for stating objectives: "The most useful form for stating objectives is to express them in terms which identify the kind of behavior to be developed in the student and the content . . . in which the behavior is to operate" (p. 30).

However, the dimensions from the two taxonomies have distinct differences. One difference is that the New Taxonomy explicitly addresses cognitive, affective, and psychomotor aspects of learning. Specifically, the psychomotor domain is one of the three knowledge domains and "examining emotional response" is a specific aspect of the self-system (see Chapter 3). As its title indicates, Bloom's original work addressed the cognitive domain. However, a taxonomy was also developed for the affective domain (see

Krathwohl, Bloom, & Masia, 1964), and the intention of Bloom and his coauthors was to develop a taxonomy for the psychomotor domain. The Anderson taxonomy does not explicitly address these distinctions. The authors explain that Bloom's Taxonomy "divided objectives into three domains: cognitive, affective, and psychomotor. This decision has been justly criticized because it isolates aspects of the same objective—and nearly every cognitive objective has an affective component" (Anderson et al., 2001, p. 258). To avoid the criticisms levied at Bloom, the Anderson taxonomy focuses on the cognitive domain: "By intentionally focusing on the cognitive domain, this revision ignores this problem" (p. 259). With this intentional focus noted, Anderson et al. concede that the Metacognitive Knowledge category of their taxonomy "in some respects bridges the cognitive and affective domains" (p. 259).

Another important difference between the New Taxonomy and Anderson's taxonomy involves the placement of metacognition. In the New Taxonomy it is placed above the cognitive processes in that goals are established by the metacognitive system, and whether one has an explicit goal (or not) within a specific learning situation can affect the type and level of cognitive processing that occurs. Thus within the New Taxonomy, metacognition represents a type of processing that is applied to subject matter content. In the Anderson et al. (2001) taxonomy, metacognition is placed in the same dimension as subject matter content, such as factual knowledge, conceptual knowledge, and procedural knowledge. Apparently the deliberation as to where meta-cognition should be situated involved a significant amount of discussion: "During the meetings that led to the preparation of this revised Taxonomy, we discussed frequently and in great detail both the inclusion and proper placement of *Metacognitive knowledge*" (p. 44). The authors further note that after they had "grappled with [the issue] for a long time" (p. 44), metacognition was placed in the knowledge dimension. It is interesting that they note that it does not fit perfectly within this category: "Of course Metacognitive knowledge does not have the same status as the other three knowledge types" (p. 44).

The third major difference in the two taxonomies is found in the treat-ment of self-system thinking. In the New Taxonomy it is placed at the top of the hierarchy because it controls whether or not a learner engages in a new task and the level of energy or motivation allotted to the task if the learner chooses to engage. In the Anderson taxonomy self-system thinking is considered an aspect of metacognitive knowledge based on Flavell's (1979) original article on the topic. While Flavell made a viable case for self-knowledge as an aspect of metacognition in 1979, since then a con-siderable amount of research and theory has established the self-system as a central aspect of human thought apart from the metacognitive system. As Csikszentmihalyi (1990) notes,

> The self is no ordinary piece of information. . . . In fact, it contains [almost] everything . . . that passes through consciousness: all the memories, actions, desires, pleasures, and pains are included in it. And more than anything else, the self represents the hierarchy of goals that we have built up, bit by bit over the years. . . . At any given time we are usually aware of only a tiny part of it. (p. 34)

In summary, while there are some similarities between the Anderson taxonomy and the New Taxonomy, there are significant differences in structure that manifest as significant differences in how the two taxonomies might be used by educators.

SUMMARY

This chapter began with a brief discussion of the nature and impact of Bloom's Taxonomy. It highlighted the problems inherent in its structure (and other adaptations and revisions) while recognizing the strength and breadth of its contribution to educational practice. A model was presented that forms the basis of the New Taxonomy. That model posits three systems of thought that have a hierarchical relationship in terms of flow of processing: the self-system, the metacognitive system, and the cognitive system.

CHAPTER TWO

The Knowledge Domains

O ne of the defining differences between Bloom's Taxonomy and the New Taxonomy is that the New Taxonomy separates various types of knowledge from the mental processes that operate on them. This is depicted in Figure 2.1.

Figure 2.1   Knowledge in the Two Taxonomies

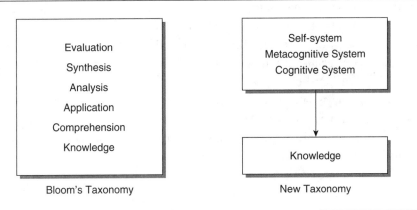

As described in Chapter 1, on the one hand, Bloom et al. (1956) defined the knowledge category within his Taxonomy as the cognitive operations of recall or recognition.

By knowledge, we mean that the student can give evidence that he remembers either by recalling or by recognizing some idea or phenomenon with which he has had experience in the educational process. For our taxonomy purposes, we are defining knowledge as little more than the remembering of the idea or phenomenon in a form very close to that in which it was originally encountered. (pp. 28–29)

On the other hand, Bloom identified specific types of knowledge within the knowledge category. These included

Terminology

Specific facts

Conventions

Trends or sequences

Classifications and categories

Criteria

Methodology

Principles and generalizations

Theories and structures

Thus within his knowledge category, Bloom included various forms of knowledge as well as the ability to recall and recognize that knowledge. This mixing of types of knowledge with the various mental operations that act on knowledge is one of the major weaknesses of Bloom's Taxonomy since, by definition, it confuses the object of an action with the action itself. In a somewhat self-accusatory manner, Bloom noted that there was a fundamental difference between his knowledge category and the other five levels. Specifically, he separated the knowledge category from the other five levels by a detailed discussion of "intellectual abilities and skills" (pp. 38, 39). Thus Bloom implicitly recognized the difference between knowledge and the mental operations that are executed on knowledge, but he mixed the two in the basic structure of his taxonomy.

The New Taxonomy avoids this confusion by postulating three domains of knowledge that are operated on by the three systems of thought and their component elements. It is the systems of thought that have the hierarchical structure that constitutes the New Taxonomy. As described in subsequent chapters, these hierarchical mental operations interact differentially with the three knowledge domains. In this chapter we consider the three knowledge domains.

KNOWLEDGE AS DOMAINS

Knowledge plays a key role in one's ability to successfully engage in a new task. Without the necessary knowledge, a student can be highly motivated to engage in the task (self-system thinking), set specific goals relative to the task (metacognitive thinking), and even bring to bear a series of keen, analytic skills (cognitive thinking). However, unless the student possesses the requisite knowledge for the task, the effects of these mental processes will be minimal.

Knowledge can be organized into three general categories: information, mental procedures, and psychomotor procedures. Any subject area can be described in terms of how much of these three types of knowledge it comprises. For example, the knowledge specific to the subject of geography includes information about various locations, weather patterns, and the influences that location has on the development of a region; the knowledge associated with geography also includes mental procedures, such as how to read and use a contour map or how to read and use a political map. There is probably little, if any, psychomotor knowledge that is specific to geography. Flying an airplane, on the other hand, requires a significant amount of psychomotor knowledge. For example, a pilot must master the physical skills involved in such activities as landing and taking off. Informational knowledge necessary to be an effective pilot would include an understanding of certain concepts, such as lift and drag. Last, the mental procedure knowledge necessary to be an effective pilot would include strategies for efficient scanning and interpreting an instrument panel.

Given the inherent differences in these types of knowledge, it is useful to think of them as related *domains* that are acted upon by the cognitive, metacognitive, and self-systems.

The Domain of Information

The domain of information, sometimes referred to as *declarative knowledge*, can be conceptualized as hierarchic in its own right. At the bottom of the informational hierarchy are vocabulary terms. A vocabulary term is a word or phrase about which a student has an accurate, but not necessarily a deep, level of understanding. For example, a student might have a general understanding of the term *probability* but not know all the nuances of the various applications of probability. This is not to say that knowledge of vocabulary is unimportant. Indeed, it is fairly obvious that students must understand a certain amount of the basic vocabulary in a subject area before they can understand the facts, generalizations, and principles within a content area (Marzano, 2004). This might explain why teachers frequently must devote a significant amount of time to vocabulary instruction. For example, after analyzing popular textbooks, Bloom (1976) concluded that textbooks commonly introduce as many as 100 to 150 new terms per chapter (p. 25).

At a level above vocabulary items are facts. Facts present information about specific persons, places, things, and events. To illustrate, "The Battle of Gettysburg was pivotal to the outcome of the Civil War" is a fact. To understand this fact, a student must understand the words (i.e., vocabulary terms) *pivotal* and *outcome*. At the top of the hierarchy are more general structures, such as generalizations and principles. The statement, "Specific battles sometimes disproportionately influence the outcome of a war," is a generalization. Although vocabulary terms and facts are important, generalizations help students develop a broad knowledge base because they transfer more readily to different situations. For instance, the preceding generalization can be applied to countries, situations, and ages, whereas the fact of the Battle of Gettysburg is a specific event that does not transfer directly to other situations. This is not to say that facts are unimportant. On the contrary, to truly understand generalizations, students must be able to support them with exemplifying facts. For example, to understand the generalization about the influences of specific battles, students need a rich set of illustrative facts, one of which could be that regarding the Battle of Gettysburg.

The various types of knowledge within the information domain are described in more detail in Figure 2.2.

Figure 2.2   Types of Informational Knowledge

Vocabulary Terms

At the most specific level of informational knowledge are vocabulary terms. In this system, knowing a vocabulary term means understanding the meaning of a word in a general way. For example, when a student understands declarative knowledge at the level of a vocabulary term, he or she has a general idea what the word means and no serious misconceptions about its meaning. To organize classroom content as vocabulary terms is to organize it as independent words and phrases. The expectation is that students have an accurate but somewhat surface-level understanding of the meaning of these terms.

Facts

Facts are a very specific type of informational content. Facts convey information about specific persons, places, living and nonliving things, and events. They commonly articulate information such as the following:

- The characteristics of a specific real or fictitious person (e.g., The fictitious character Robin Hood first appeared in English literature in the early 1800s.)
- The characteristics of a specific place (e.g., Denver is in the state of Colorado.)
- The characteristics of specific living and nonliving things (e.g., My dog, Tuffy, is a golden retriever; the Empire State Building is over 100 stories high.)
- The characteristics of a specific event (e.g., Construction began on the Leaning Tower of Pisa in 1174.)

Time Sequences

Time sequences include important events that occurred between two points in time. For example, the events that occurred between President Kennedy's assassination on November 22, 1963, and his burial on November 25, 1963, are organized as a time sequence in most people's memories. First one thing happened, then another, then another. As described in the section on principles, time sequences can include some elements that have a causal relationship.

Generalizations

Generalizations are statements for which examples can be provided. For example, the statement, "U.S. presidents often come from families that have great wealth or influence," is a generalization, for which examples can be provided. It is easy to confuse some generalizations with some facts. Facts identify characteristics of *specific* persons, places, living and nonliving things, and events, whereas generalizations identify characteristics about *classes* or *categories* of persons, places, living and nonliving things, and events. For example, the statement, "My dog, Tuffy, is a golden retriever" is a fact. However, the statement, "Golden retrievers are good hunters," is a generalization. In addition, generalizations identify characteristics about abstractions. Specifically, information about abstractions is always stated in the form of generalizations. Examples of the various types of generalizations follow:

- Characteristics of classes of persons (e.g., It takes at least two years of training to become a fireman.)
- Characteristics of classes of places (e.g., Large cities have high crime rates.)
- Characteristics of classes of living and nonliving things (e.g., Golden retrievers are good hunting dogs; firearms are the subject of great debate.)
- Characteristics of classes of events (e.g., The Super Bowl is a premier sporting event each year.)
- Characteristics of abstractions (e.g., Love is one of the most powerful human emotions.)

Principles

Principles are specific types of generalizations that deal with relationships. In general, there are two types of principles found in school-related declarative knowledge: *cause-effect principles* and *correlational principles.*

Cause-effect principles. Cause-effect principles articulate causal relationships. For example, the sentence, "Tuberculosis is caused by the tubercle bacillus," is a cause-effect principle. Although not stated here, understanding a cause-effect principle includes knowledge of the specific elements within the system and the exact relationships those elements have to one another. That is, to understand the cause-effect principle regarding tuberculosis and the bacterium, one would have to understand the sequence of events that occur, the elements involved, and the type and strength of the relationships between those elements. In short, understanding a cause-effect principle involves a great deal of information.

Correlational principles. Correlational principles describe relationships that are not necessarily causal in nature but in which a change in one factor is associated with a change in another factor. For example, the following is a correlational principle: "The increase in lung cancer among women is directly proportional to the increase in the number of women who smoke."

Again, to understand this principle, a student would have to know the specific details about this relationship. Specifically, a student would have to know the general pattern of this relationship, that is, the number of women who have lung cancer changes at the same rate as the changes in the number of women who smoke.

These two types of principles are sometimes confused with time *sequences* that involve cause-effect relationships. A cause-effect sequence applies to a specific situation, whereas a principle applies to many situations. The causes of the Civil War taken together represent a time sequence with some causal relationships. They apply to the Civil War only. However, the cause-effect principle linking tuberculosis and the tubercle bacillus can be applied to many different situations and many different people. Physicians use this principle to make judgments about a variety of situations and a variety of people. The key distinction between principles and cause-effect sequences is that principles can be exemplified in a number of situations, whereas cause-effect sequences cannot: They apply to a single situation only.

Those familiar with the literature on types of information might notice that Figure 2.2 does not list concepts, although they are frequently listed in other discussions (see Carroll, 1964; Klausmeier, 1985; Klausmeier & Sipple, 1980; Tennyson & Cocchiarella, 1986). This is because concepts, as described by other theorists, are basically synonymous with generalizations as described in this work. To illustrate, Gagne (1977) describes a concept as "a particular kind of rule, a rule that classifies" (p. 134). As described in Figure 2.2, this is a defining feature of generalizations. Concepts, then, as discussed in other works, are basically identical with what is defined as a generalization or principle in the New Taxonomy.

Although there are many components in the informational domain, ranging from vocabulary terms to different types of principles, it is appropriate and useful for the purpose of the New Taxonomy to organize the types of information into two broad categories: details and organizing ideas. Details include vocabulary terms, facts, and time sequences; organizing ideas include generalizations and principles. This is depicted as follows:

Details
  Vocabulary terms
  Facts
  Time sequences

Organizing ideas
  Principles
  Generalizations

As demonstrated in subsequent chapters, the three systems of thought—cognitive, metacognitive, and self-systems—interact in the same way within these two categories, but somewhat differently between categories. That is, the processes within the cognitive system apply to time sequences in the same way that they apply to facts since both are details. Similarly, the processes within the cognitive system apply to principles in the same way they apply to generalizations since both are organizing ideas. However, the processes within the cognitive system do not apply to generalizations the same way they apply to time sequences.

A final characteristic of informational knowledge important to a discussion of the New Taxonomy is the manner in which it is represented in memory. Some psychologists assert that informational knowledge exists in memory in propositional form. The construct of a proposition has a rich history in both psychology and linguistics (Frederiksen, 1975; Kintsch, 1974; Norman & Rumelhart, 1975). In simple terms, "a proposition is the smallest unit of thought that can stand as a separate assertion, that is, the smallest unit about which it makes sense to make the judgment true or false" (Anderson, 1990b, p.123). Clark and Clark (1977) have noted that there is a finite set of the types of propositions. Figure 2.3 depicts the major types.

Figure 2.3   Major Types of Propositions

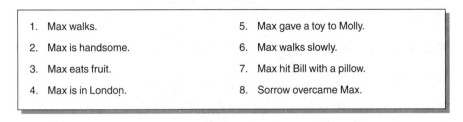

1. Max walks.	5. Max gave a toy to Molly.
2. Max is handsome.	6. Max walks slowly.
3. Max eats fruit.	7. Max hit Bill with a pillow.
4. Max is in London.	8. Sorrow overcame Max.

Each of the statements in Figure 2.3 can be affirmed or denied, yet none of their component parts can. That is, one could determine if it is true that Max walks or Max is handsome, but one could not confirm or deny *Max, walks, is,* or *handsome* in isolation. Propositions, then, might be described as the most basic form in which information is stored.

Propositions are combined in networks to form complex information. For example, Figure 2.4 represents the propositional network for the statements, "Bill went to the drugstore where he met his sister. They bought their father a coat."

Figure 2.4   Propositional Network

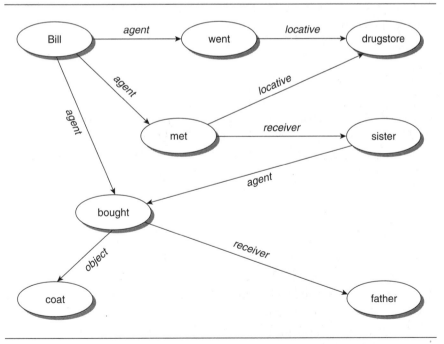

Note that the lines in Figure 2.4 are labeled *agent, object, locative,* and *receiver*. These represent the various types of relationships that can exist between propositions and between the elements within propositions.

(For discussions of the types of relationships in propositional networks, see Chafe, 1970; Fillmore, 1968; and Turner & Greene, 1977.)

THE DOMAIN OF MENTAL PROCEDURES

Mental procedures—sometimes referred to as *procedural knowledge*—are different in form and function from information or declarative knowledge. The distinction between declarative and procedural knowledge is considered basic by some psychologists. For example, psychologists Snow and Lohman (1989) note that "the distinction between declarative and procedural knowledge, or more simply, content knowledge and process knowledge" is one of the most basic in terms of guiding educational practice (p. 266).

Whereas declarative knowledge can be considered the "what" of human knowledge, procedural knowledge can be described as the "how-to." For example, an individual's knowledge about how to drive a car or how to do long division is procedural in nature. Again, the format in which procedures are stored in memory is highly relevant to the discussion of the New Taxonomy.

Psychologist John Anderson (1983) has described the basic nature of procedural knowledge as if-then structures called *productions*. The structure of productions is different from the structure of propositional networks. To illustrate, the following is part of the production network for the procedure of multicolumn subtraction:

1a.	*If* the goal is to do multicolumn subtraction,	1b.	*Then* make the goal to process the right-most column.
2a.	*If* there is an answer in the current column and there is a column to the left,	2b.	*Then* make the goal to process the column to the left.
3a.	*If* the goal is to process a column and there is no bottom digit or the bottom digit is zero,	3b.	*Then* record the top digit as the answer, and so on.

In its entirety, this production network would have scores of if-then pairs—scores of productions. (For a complete discussion of production networks, see Anderson, 1983, 1990a, 1990b, and 1995.) Knowledge within the domain of mental procedures, then, is different in structure from knowledge within the domain of information.

Another important feature of knowledge in the domain of mental procedures as it relates to the New Taxonomy is the manner in which it is learned. Specifically, there are three relatively distinct phases to the acquisition of mental procedures. Fitts (1964) calls the first the *cognitive* stage. At this point, the learner can verbalize the process (describe it, if asked) and might be able to perform at least a crude approximation of the procedure. According to Anderson (1983), it is common to observe verbal "mediation" during which the learner rehearses the information required to execute the skill. In the second stage, called the *associative* stage, the performance of the procedure is smoothed out. At this juncture, errors in the initial understanding of the procedure are detected and deleted along with the need for verbal rehearsal. During the third stage, the *autonomous* stage, the procedure is refined. It is at this level that the procedure becomes automatic (LaBerge & Samuels, 1974); the procedure once called to mind by the learner is automatically executed and takes very little of the available space in working memory.

These phases of acquisition are important to the New Taxonomy because procedural knowledge acquired at the cognitive stage is, for all practical purposes, identical with information knowledge. To illustrate, at the first stage of learning multicolumn subtraction, students might be able to describe the procedure and even answer questions about it, but they might not actually be able to perform it. Thus even though the procedure has a production structure, it is understood by learners in the same way they would understand informational knowledge. As we shall see in subsequent chapters, this characteristic of procedural knowledge has implications for how it is acted upon by the mental processes within the various levels of the New Taxonomy.

Like the domain of information, the domain of mental procedures can be organized into a simple hierarchy. At the top of the hierarchy are highly robust procedures that have a diversity of possible products or outcomes and involve the execution of many interrelated subprocedures. Technically, such operations are referred to as *macroprocedures* (Marzano & Kendall, 1996a). The prefix *macro* indicates that the procedure is highly complex, having many subcomponents that require some form of management. For example, the procedure of writing fulfills the defining characteristics of a macroprocedure. Different students writing on the same topic will produce very different compositions even though they are addressing the same topic and executing the same steps.

Somewhat in the middle of the hierarchy are mental procedures that do not generate the variety of products possible from macroprocedures and do not incorporate the wide variety of subcomponents. These procedures are commonly referred to as *tactics* (see Snowman & McCown, 1984). For example, an individual may have a tactic for reading a histogram. Tactics do not consist of a set of steps that must be performed in a specific order. Rather, they are made up of general rules with an overall flow of execution. For example, a tactic for reading a histogram might include rules that address (a) identifying the elements depicted in the legend, (b) determining what is reported in each axis on the graph, and (c) determining the relationship between the elements on the two axes. Although there is a general pattern in which these rules are executed, there is no rigid or set order.

Algorithms are mental procedures that normally do not vary in application once learned. They have very specific outcomes and very specific steps. The previous example of multicolumn subtraction is an illustration of an algorithm. Algorithms must be learned to the level of automaticity to be useful.

The simplest type of mental procedure is a *single rule* or a small set of rules with no accompanying steps. A single rule would consist of one if-then production—*If* situation *X* occurs, *then* perform action *Y*. Single-rule mental procedures are commonly employed in sets. For example, students who know five rules for capitalization might apply these independently while editing their writing; they would be using a group of single-rule procedures. If the students systematically executed the rules in a set sequence, however (e.g., check capitalization at the beginning of each sentence first, next check the capitalization of proper nouns, and so on), they would have organized the single-rule procedures into a tactic or algorithm, depending on how rigidly the pattern of execution was followed.

For the purpose of the New Taxonomy, it is useful to organize the domain of mental procedures into two broad categories: (1) those that, with practice, can be executed automatically or with little conscious thought and (2) those that must be controlled. Tactics, algorithms, and single rules can be learned to the level of automaticity or to the level of little conscious thought. Macroprocedures, by definition, require controlled execution. As a set, tactics, algorithms, and single rules will be referred to as skills; macroprocedures will be referred to simply as processes. Thus as Figure 2.5 depicts, the two categories of mental procedures within the New Taxonomy are *processes* and *skills*.

Figure 2.5   Categories of Mental Procedures

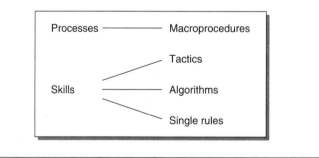

THE DOMAIN OF PSYCHOMOTOR PROCEDURES

As the name implies, the psychomotor domain is composed of physical procedures an individual uses to negotiate daily life and to engage in complex physical activities for work and for recreation. It should be noted that Bloom et al. (1956) originally intended to address psychomotor skills as a separate domain. However, the document describing this domain was never published by Bloom and his colleagues.

Why is the psychomotor domain considered a type of knowledge in the New Taxonomy? Psychomotor procedures are considered a type of knowledge for two reasons. First, they are stored in memory in a fashion identical with mental procedures: They are stored as if-then production networks (Anderson, 1983). Second, the stages of development for acquiring psychomotor procedures are similar to, if not identical with, those involved in acquiring mental procedures (Anderson, 1983, 1995; Gagne, 1977, 1989): They are first learned as information, during initial practice they are shaped, and then finally they are learned to a level of automaticity or near automaticity.

As is the case with the other two domains, the psychomotor domain can be organized into a hierarchy. At the bottom are foundational physical abilities upon which more complex procedures are developed. Carroll (1993) has identified a number of these foundational abilities, which include

Static strength

Overall body equilibrium

Speed of limb movement

Wrist-finger speed

Finger dexterity

Manual dexterity

Arm-hand steadiness

Control precision

It is clear from this listing that these procedures are generally developed without formal instruction. Indeed, human beings perform all these physical functions naturally with a certain degree of acumen. However, this is not to say that these foundational skills cannot be improved with instruction and practice. For example, with instruction, a person's manual dexterity can be improved. Therefore, they qualify as types of knowledge in that they can be enhanced through instruction.

At a level up from basic foundational procedures are simple combination procedures, such as shooting a free throw in basketball. As their name implies, simple combination procedures involve sets of foundational procedures acting in parallel. For example, shooting a free throw is an example of a simple combination procedure that involves the interaction of a number of foundational procedures, such as wrist-finger speed, control precision, and arm-hand steadiness.

Last, complex combination procedures use sets of simple combination procedures. For example, the act of playing defense in basketball would involve the combination skills of side-to-side movement with the body in a squatting position, hand waving, and so on. Thus what is commonly thought of as a sport or a recreational activity can be operationally defined as the use of a set of complex combination procedures for the purpose of accomplishing specific physical goals (e.g., hitting a ball over a net within prescribed boundaries while using a specific type of racquet).

Again, for purposes of the New Taxonomy, it is useful to organize the procedures in the psychomotor domain into two categories. This is illustrated in Figure 2.6.

In summary, for the purposes of the New Taxonomy, the components in the three domains of knowledge have been organized as depicted in Figure 2.7.

Figure 2.6   Categories of Psychomotor Procedures

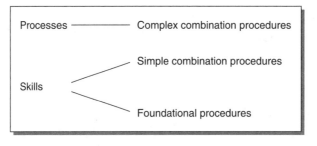

Figure 2.7   Components of the Three Knowledge Domains

Information	1. Organizing ideas	Principles Generalizations
	2. Details	Time sequences Facts Vocabulary terms
Mental Procedures	1. Processes	Macroprocedures
	2. Skills	Tactics Algorithms Single rules
Psychomotor Procedures	1. Processes	Complex combination procedures
	2. Skills	Simple combination procedures Foundational procedures

RELATIONSHIP TO BLOOM'S TAXONOMY

To recap, the convention employed in the New Taxonomy of considering knowledge as that which is acted upon by various mental processes is a significant departure from Bloom's Taxonomy. Another significant difference is the New Taxonomy's inclusion of psychomotor procedures as a type of knowledge akin to mental procedures and information. One similarity, however, between the New Taxonomy and Bloom's Taxonomy is their respective delineations of informational types. Both place terms and phrases at the lower end of the information hierarchy and generalizations and principles at the higher end.

SUMMARY

This chapter has described three domains of knowledge: (1) information, (2) mental procedures, and (3) psychomotor procedures. Whereas information is stored as propositional networks, mental and psychomotor procedures are stored as production networks. The components within each of the three domains are organized into two categories. The informational domain is subdivided into details and organizing ideas. The domains of mental procedures and psychomotor procedures are organized into skills and processes.

CHAPTER THREE

The Three Systems of Thinking

The three systems of thought introduced in Chapter 1 are at the heart of the New Taxonomy. As we have seen, these three systems—the self-system, the metacognitive system, and the cognitive system—can be ordered hierarchically. In addition, as is explained at the end of this chapter, the four elements of the cognitive system can be ordered hierarchically within that system. This makes for a six-tiered taxonomy as depicted in Figure 3.1, which represents the basic structure of the New Taxonomy.

Figure 3.1   Six Levels of the New Taxonomy

Level 6: Self-system

Level 5: Metacognitive System

Level 4: Knowledge Utilization

Level 3: Analysis

Level 2: Comprehension

Level 1: Retrieval

Cognitive System

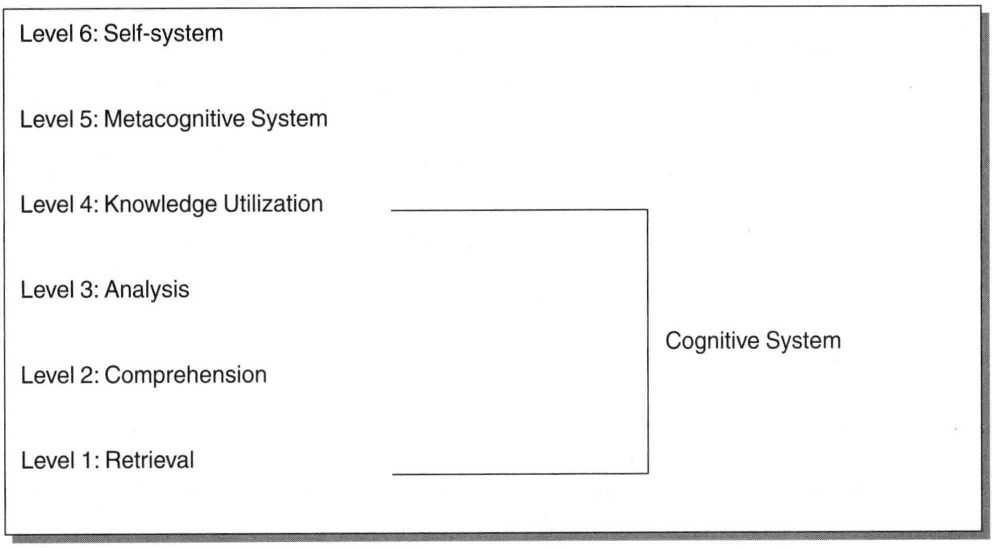

MEMORY

To be able to discuss the six levels of the New Taxonomy in detail, it is first necessary to consider briefly the nature and function of memory. There have been many models proposed for the nature and function of human memory. Anderson (1995) explains that the long-held conception of two types of memory—short term and long term—has been replaced with the theory that there is only one type of memory, with different functions. For the purpose of this discussion, we consider three functions: sensory memory, permanent memory, and working memory.

Sensory memory deals with the temporary storage of data from the senses. Anderson (1995) describes sensory memory in the following way:

> Sensory memory is capable of storing more or less complete records of what has been encountered for brief periods of time, during which people can note relationships among the elements and encode the elements in a more permanent memory. If the information in sensory memory is not encoded in the brief time before it decays, it is lost. What subjects encode depends on what they are paying attention to. The environment typically offers much more information at one time than we can attend to and encode. Therefore, much of what enters our sensory system results in no permanent record. (p. 160)

Permanent memory contains all information, organizing ideas, skills, and processes that constitute the domains of knowledge. In short, all that we understand and know how to do is stored in permanent memory.

Working memory uses data from both sensory memory and permanent memory. As its name implies, working memory is where data are actively processed. This is depicted in Figure 3.2.

Figure 3.2   Types of Memory

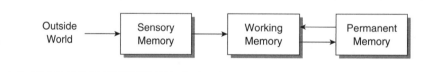

As shown in Figure 3.2, working memory can receive data from sensory memory (where it is held only briefly), from permanent memory (where it resides permanently), or from both. There is no theoretical limit on the amount of time data can reside in working memory. As long as an individual focuses conscious attention on the data in working memory, the data stay active. To this extent, working memory can be considered the seat of consciousness: Our experience of consciousness is actually our experience of what is being processed in working memory (Dennett, 1969, 1991).

LEVEL 1: RETRIEVAL (COGNITIVE SYSTEM)

Having a basic understanding of the construct of working memory, we can describe retrieval as the activation and transfer of knowledge from permanent memory to working memory, where it might be consciously processed. Retrieval is a process within the cognitive system and is, of course, an innate process—it is part of every human's neurological "hard-wiring." It is generally done without conscious awareness by an individual.

The actual process of retrieval is somewhat different depending upon the type of knowledge involved and the degree of processing required. In the New Taxonomy, retrieval of information is either a matter of *recognition* or *recall*. This distinction has a long history in the psychological literature (see, for example, Spearman, 1927) and has empirical support (Laufer & Goldstein, 2004). Recognition can be defined as the simple matching of a given prompt or stimulus with information in permanent memory. Recall, by contrast, requires some level of recognition and in addition, the production of related information. For example, a student who selects a synonym from among a set of words relies upon recognition. A student asked to define a word or produce a synonym employs recall. In addition to recognizing the term, the student must produce an appropriate response. This distinction constitutes a hierarchy of difficulty within Level I of the New Taxonomy.

Another way of understanding the distinction between recognition and recall is to note that when information is retrieved from permanent memory, it often is associated with more than a simple matching of information at the level of recognition. The information retrieved contains additional components that may not have been explicit in the student's initial learning experience. Human beings naturally elaborate on information taken into working memory, and this elaboration is available for later recall. To illustrate, assume that an individual hears the following information as a part of a discussion with someone:

> The two young girls, Mary and Sally, saw the book of matches and immediately began thinking of games to play. By midafternoon the house was engulfed in flames.

In a strictly logical sense, this information is incomplete. There is no statement as to the direct relationship between the games the children played and the fire. To make sense of what was explicitly stated, an individual would necessarily infer missing information, such as this sequence: The children began playing with the matches; their game caught the house on fire. In working memory, the implicit information would be enhanced to produce a coherent whole such as the following:

Proposition 1: The two young girls, Mary and Sally, saw the matches (stated).

Proposition 2: The children began thinking of games (stated).

Proposition 3: The games included using the matches (inferred).

Proposition 4: While the children were playing games with the matches, the house caught on fire (inferred).

Proposition 5: The fire was accidental (inferred).

Proposition 6: The house caught on fire in the early afternoon (inferred).

Proposition 7: By midafternoon the house was engulfed in flames (stated).

Proposition 8: The house was destroyed or severely damaged (inferred).

Some researchers have referred to this more logically complete version of the information as a "microstructure" (Turner & Greene, 1977). Obviously, inference plays a major role in the design of a complete microstructure. There are two basic types of inferences made when constructing a microstructure: default inferences and reasoned inferences. Default inferences are those you commonly make about people, places, things, events, and abstractions (de Beaugrande, 1980; Kintsch, 1979; van Dijk, 1980). For example, when you read the sentence, "Bill had a dog," you immediately add information such as "The dog had four legs," "The dog liked to eat bones," "The dog liked to be petted," and so on. In other words, you have information stored about dogs. In the absence of information to the contrary, you infer that this general information is true about the dog, even though it is not explicitly mentioned in the text.

Reasoned inferences are another way we add information that is not explicit. Such inferences are not part of our general knowledge. Rather, they are reasoned conclusions. For example, if you read the statement, "Experimental psychologists believe that you have to test generalizations to see if they are true," and later read about a psychologist who is presented with a new theory by a colleague, you will naturally conclude that the psychologist will probably suggest that the theory be tested. This inference comes not from your general knowledge base about psychologists but is induced from the earlier information you read about experimental psychologists.

Although knowledge from the domain of information is only recognized or recalled, knowledge from the domains of mental procedures and psychomotor procedures can be *executed* as well. As explained in Chapter 2, procedures of all types have an if-then structure, referred to as productions.

When the steps in these productions are carried out, something occurs and a product results. For example, in the case of the production described in the previous chapter regarding multicolumn subtraction, a quantity is computed when the steps are carried out. Thus we say that *procedural knowledge is executed*, whereas *information is recognized and recalled*. However, it is also true that procedural knowledge can be recognized and recalled, because all procedures have embedded information. To illustrate, reconsider the first part of the production network for the procedure of multicolumn subtraction:

1a. *If* the goal is to do multicolumn subtraction,

1b. *Then* make the goal to process the right-most column.

2a. *If* there is an answer in the current column and there is a column to the left,

2b. *Then* make the goal to process the column to the left.

3a. *If* the goal is to process a column and there is no bottom digit or the bottom digit is zero,

3b. *Then* record the top digit as the answer.

Notice that to execute this procedure effectively, a student would have to understand some basic information, such as

The number in the right-most column represents ones.

The number in the next column to the left represents tens.

The number in the next column to the left represents hundreds, and so on.

Procedures, then, commonly include information that must be understood so that the procedure can be executed effectively. For this reason, procedures—or at least the information embedded within them—can be recognized and recalled. However, by its very nature, a procedure must be executed to be fully employed.

Relationship to Bloom's Taxonomy

As defined in the New Taxonomy, the cognitive process of retrieval is akin to the knowledge level in Bloom's Taxonomy. Again, Bloom and his colleagues (1956) described his knowledge category in the following way: "For our taxonomy purposes, we are defining knowledge as little more than remembering the idea or phenomenon in a form very close to that in which it was originally encountered" (pp. 28–29). In addition, Bloom explained that "knowledge as defined here includes those behaviors and test situations which emphasize the remembering, either by recognition or recall, of ideas, material, or phenomena" (p. 62). Although most of Bloom's examples within his knowledge level deal with information only, one might infer from some of his examples that by knowledge he also means the execution of mental procedures. Again, it is worth noting that Bloom confounded the object of retrieval (i.e., knowledge) with the processes of retrieval (i.e., recall and execution). The New Taxonomy does not.

LEVEL 2: COMPREHENSION (COGNITIVE SYSTEM)

The process of comprehension within the cognitive system is responsible for translating knowledge into a form appropriate for storage in permanent memory. That is, data that are deposited in working memory via sensory memory are not stored in permanent memory exactly as experienced. We have seen that the learner quite naturally infers implicit information via default and reasoned inferences. However, to store the information in permanent memory in an efficient manner, it must be translated into a structure and format that preserves the key information, as opposed to extraneous information. The extent to which an individual has stored knowledge in this parsimonious fashion is the extent to which the individual has comprehended that knowledge. In short, the process of comprehension in the New Taxonomy involves storing the critical features of information in permanent memory.

Comprehension, as defined in the New Taxonomy, involves two related processes: integrating and symbolizing.

Integrating

Integrating is the process of distilling knowledge down to its key characteristics, organized in a parsimonious, generalized form—technically referred to as a macrostructure, as opposed to a microstructure (Kintsch, 1974, 1979; van Dijk, 1977, 1980). Whereas the microstructure contains information acquired from direct experience and inference, the macrostructure contains the gist of the information in the microstructure. By definition, the process of integration involves the mixing of new knowledge recently experienced by the learner and old knowledge residing in the learner's permanent memory. This integration is accomplished via the application of rules technically referred to as *macrorules*. For example, van Dijk and Kintsch (1983) have identified three macrorules that are used to translate a microstructure into a macrostructure:

1. Deletion: Given a sequence of propositions, delete any proposition that is not directly related to the other propositions in the sequence.

2. Generalization: Replace any proposition with one that includes the information in a more general form.

3. Construction: Replace any set of propositions with one or more that include the information in the set stated in more general terms.

When applied appropriately, these rules generate a parsimonious representation of information that does not include all details but includes the general outline of the critical information. This explains why individuals usually do not remember the specific facts in an interesting story they have read but do tend to recall the general flow of information and events.

Evidence that students have effectively integrated knowledge is that they can produce the macrostructure for that knowledge—a statement of the important or critical elements of that knowledge.

Symbolizing

Symbolizing is the comprehension process of creating a symbolic analog of the knowledge contained in a macrostructure. The concept of symbolizing as a mental process is grounded in dual-coding theories of knowledge, such as that articulated by Paivio (1969, 1971). According to that theory, information is processed into two primary modes: linguistic and imagery. The linguistic mode is semantic in nature and, as we have seen, is expressed as propositions or productions. One might think of the linguistic mode as containing actual statements in permanent memory. The imagery code, in contrast, is expressed as mental pictures or even physical sensations, such as smell, taste, touch, kinesthetic association, and sound (Richardson, 1983).

Symbolizing, then, is the translation of the knowledge contained in a macrostructure into some symbolic imagery (i.e., nonlinguistic) mode. Hayes (1981) provides an example of the representation process, using the following equation from physics:

$$F = \frac{(M1 \times M2)G}{r^2}$$

The equation states that force (F) is equal to the product of the masses of two objects ($M1$ and $M2$) times a constant (G), divided by the square of the distance between them (r). There are a number of ways this information might be represented symbolically. Hayes (1981) suggests an image of two large globes in space with the learner in the middle trying to hold them apart:

> If either of the globes were very heavy, we would expect that it would be harder to hold them apart than if both were light. Since force increases as either of the masses (M's) increases, the masses must be in the numerator. As we push the globes further apart, the force of attraction between them will decrease as the force of attraction between two magnets decreases as we pull them apart. Since force decreases as distance increases, r must be in the denominator. (p. 127)

A popular form of symbolizing in K–12 classrooms is graphic organizers, which combine language and symbols. Examples of how graphic organizers can be used across different content areas have been offered by Clarke (1991), Heimlich and Pittelman (1988), Jones, Palincsar, Ogle, and Carr (1987), and McTighe and Lyman (1988). Some assert that most informational knowledge can be symbolized using a very small set of organizational patterns. Combining the work of Cooper (1983), Frederiksen (1977), and Meyer (1975) yields a number of popular organizational patterns such as the following:

- *Characteristic patterns* organize facts or characteristics about specific persons, places, things, and events. The characteristics need be in no particular order. For example, information in a film about the state of Colorado—its location, its altitude, specific events that occurred there—might be organized as a simple descriptive pattern.
- *Sequence patterns* organize events in a specific chronological order. For example, a chapter in a book relating the events that occurred during the 1999 war in Kosovo might be organized as a sequence pattern.
- *Process-cause patterns* organize information into a causal network leading to a specific outcome or into a sequence of steps leading to a specific product. For example, information about the events leading to the war in Kosovo might be organized as a process-cause pattern.
- *Problem-solution patterns* organize information into an identified problem and its possible solutions. For example, information about the various types of diction errors that might occur in an essay and the ways of correcting those errors might be organized as a problem-solution pattern.
- *Generalization patterns* organize information into a generalization with supporting examples. For example, a chapter in a textbook about U.S. presidents might be organized using this generalization: "U.S. presidents frequently come from influential families." It would be followed by examples of specific presidents.

Each of these patterns lends itself to a particular type of graphic organizer. These organizers are depicted in Figure 3.3.

Figure 3.3   Graphic Representations for Patterns

Characteristic Pattern

Sequence Pattern

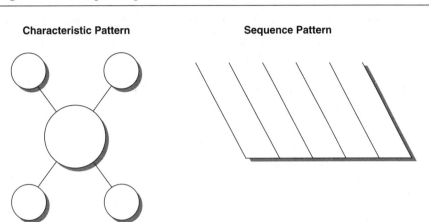

Process-Cause Pattern

Problem-Solution Pattern

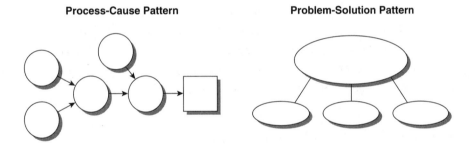

Generalization Pattern

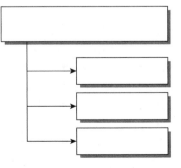

Relationship to Bloom's Taxonomy

Comprehension as defined in the New Taxonomy is fairly similar to comprehension as defined in Bloom's Taxonomy. Bloom et al. (1956) describe comprehension in the following way:

> Here we are using the term "comprehension" to include those *objectives, behaviors,* or *responses* which represent an understanding of the literal message contained in a communication. In reaching such an understanding, the student may change the communication in his mind or in his overt responses to some parallel form more meaningful to him. There may also be responses which represent simple extensions beyond what is given in the communication itself. (p. 89)

As discussed, Bloom's Taxonomy identifies three types of comprehension: translation, interpretation, and extrapolation. *Translation* is basically synonymous with *symbolizing* in the New Taxonomy since both involve encoding knowledge in a form different from that in which it was initially perceived. However, symbolizing in the New Taxonomy appears to emphasize symbolic and nonlinguistic forms more than does translation in Bloom's Taxonomy. *Interpretation* in Bloom's Taxonomy appears synonymous with *integration* in the New Taxonomy, since both deal with addressing the knowledge as a whole or the gist of the knowledge. *Extrapolation* in Bloom's Taxonomy, however, deals with inferences that appear to go beyond the comprehension processes in the New Taxonomy.

LEVEL 3: ANALYSIS (COGNITIVE SYSTEM)

Analysis in the New Taxonomy involves the reasoned extension of knowledge. As a function of applying the analysis processes, an individual elaborates on the knowledge as comprehended. These elaborations extend far beyond the localized inferences made when knowledge is initially deposited in working memory in its microstructure format. Analysis also goes beyond the identification of essential versus nonessential characteristics that are a function of the process of comprehension. Analysis within the New Taxonomy involves the generation of new information not already possessed by the individual.

There are five analysis processes: (1) matching, (2) classifying, (3) analyzing errors, (4) generalizing, and (5) specifying. It should be noted that each of these cognitive operations can be—and frequently are—engaged in naturally without conscious thought. However, when used as analysis tools as defined in the New Taxonomy, they are executed both consciously and rigorously. When applied in this manner, these processes force the learner to cycle through knowledge many times, changing it and refining it.

Many researchers attest to this dynamic of human learning. For example, Piaget (1971) described two basic types of learning: one in which information is integrated into the learner's existing knowledge base, called *assimilation,* and another in which existing knowledge structures are changed, called *accommodation.* Other researchers and theorists have made similar distinctions. For example, Rumelhart and Norman (1981) described three basic types of learning. The first two, called *accretion* and *tuning,* deal with the gradual accumulation or addition of information over time and the expression of that information in more parsimonious ways. The third type of learning, called *restructuring,* involves reorganizing information so that it can produce new insights and be used in new situations. It is this type of learning, described by Piaget as accommodation and by Rumelhart and Norman as restructuring, that is referred to as analysis in the New Taxonomy.

Matching

Matching processes address the identification of similarities and differences between knowledge components. This is perhaps the most basic of all aspects of information processing (Smith & Medin, 1981). Matching is fundamental to most, if not all, other types of analysis processes. Researcher Arthur Markman and his colleagues have determined that, of the two aspects of matching, identifying similarities is the more primary, since without the identification of similarities, no differences can be discerned (Gentner & Markman, 1994; Markman & Gentner, 1993a, 1993b; Medin, Goldstone, & Markman, 1995).

The process of matching may be simple or complex, depending on the demands of the task (Mandler, 1983). For example, a young child will easily and naturally notice the similarities between two dogs while walking in the park. However, that child might have difficulty when asked to compare the same two dogs on characteristics that are key features of their respective breeds and explain how these similarities and differences help that breed. It is the latter form of the task that is referred to here as matching. Stahl (1985) and Beyer (1988) have noted that the following are critical characteristics of effective matching:

- Specifying the attributes or characteristics on which items being matched are to be analyzed
- Determining how they are alike and different
- Stating similarities and differences as precisely as possible

Classifying

Classifying refers to organizing knowledge into meaningful categories. Like matching, it is basic to human thought. As Mervis (1980) notes, the world is composed of an infinite number of stimuli. People make the unfamiliar familiar by organizing the myriad stimuli that bombard their senses into like categories. Indeed, Nickerson, Perkins, and Smith (1985) note that the ability to form categories of like stimuli is central to all forms of thought.

Although learners use the process of classification naturally, when used as an analytic tool, this process can be very challenging. Marzano (1992) and others (Beyer, 1988; Jones, Amiran, & Katims, 1985; Taba, 1967) have identified the following as critical attributes of effective classification:

- Identifying the defining characteristics of the items to be classified
- Identifying a superordinate category to which the item belongs and explaining why it belongs in that category
- Identifying one or more (if any) subordinate categories for the item and explaining how they are related

Analyzing Errors

Analyzing errors addresses the logic, reasonableness, or accuracy of knowledge. The existence of this cognitive function implies that information must be considered reasonable for an individual to accept it as valid (Gilovich, 1991). To illustrate, assume that a student is engaged in reading an article on a given topic. As the incoming information is being represented in working memory, the new knowledge is screened to determine if it makes sense relative to what is already known about the topic. If the information is considered illogical or unreasonable, then it will be either tagged as such prior to being stored in permanent memory, or it will be rejected. People naturally and quickly make judgments regarding how reasonable knowledge is. However, analyzing errors as an analytic skill within the New Taxonomy involves (1) consciously judging the validity of the knowledge based on explicit criteria and (2) identifying any errors in reasoning that have been presented.

To perform this function well, a student must have a basic (but not necessarily technical) understanding of the nature of evidence and well-formed arguments. Toulmin, Rieke, and Janik (1981) have identified the specifics of what students must know to make sound judgments regarding validity. This is summarized in Figure 3.4.

A student does not have to understand the technical aspects of grounds, warrants, backing, and qualifiers, such as their names and defining characteristics. However, students should be aware that to be valid, claims should be supported (grounds), the sources of the support should be identified (warrants), the support should be explained and discussed (backing), and exceptions to the claims should be identified (qualifiers).

Figure 3.4 Arguments and Evidence

---

1. Grounds: Once a claim is made, it is usually supported by grounds. Depending on the type of claim made, grounds may be composed of

   - Matters of common knowledge
   - Expert opinion
   - Previously established information
   - Experimental observation
   - Other information considered factual

   (e.g., "Evidence for Hemingway's superiority can be found in reviews of his works by expert literary critic Ralph Johnson.").

---

2. Warrants: Warrants specify or interpret the information in the grounds. Where grounds specify the source of support for a claim and the general nature of the support, warrants provide a detailed analysis of the information highlighted by grounds

   (e.g., "In one of Johnson's articles he notes that Hemingway's work exemplifies the first principle of good writing, namely, that it should stir the emotions of the reader.").

---

3. Backing: Backing establishes the validity of warrants. Warrants in and of themselves might not be wholly trusted. Consequently, it is often appropriate for there to be some discussion of the validity or general acceptance of the warrants used

   (e.g., "The principle cited by Johnson in his critique of Hemingway is one of the most frequently cited. In fact, Pearlson notes that . . .").

---

4. Qualifiers: Not all warrants lead to their claims with the same degree of certainty. Consequently, qualifiers articulate the degree of certainty for the claim or qualifiers to the claim

   (e.g., "It should be noted that Hemingway's expertise is not appreciated by all . . .").

The foregoing discussion applies to error analysis involving information. When the focus is on mental or psychomotor processes, analyzing errors is a quite different matter. To understand, consider the mental procedure of multicolumn subtraction. Brown and Burton (1978) observed a middle school student produce the following two errors:

$$
\begin{array}{r} 500 \\ -\,65 \\ \hline 565 \end{array}
\qquad
\begin{array}{r} 312 \\ -\,243 \\ \hline 149 \end{array}
$$

According to Anderson (1990b), a common response to these errors is that the student has been careless or knows very little about multicolumn subtraction. However, Brown and Burton (1978) explain that the student was actually faithfully following a self-constructed rule: $0 - N = N$; that is, "if a digit is subtracted from 0, the result is the digit." The infusion of systematic errors like this into a procedure is referred to as a *bug*. Brown and Burton found 110 such bugs students had introduced into the subtraction process.

Mental and psychomotor procedures are highly susceptible to bugs, particularly in the initial stages of learning them. The Mathematical Science Education Board (1990) has warned that when procedural knowledge is taught as a set of steps only, it does not necessarily enhance competence in the procedure. Similarly, Clement, Lockhead, and Mink (1979) have shown that even a seemingly solid understanding of the steps involved in algebraic procedures does not in most cases (over 80 percent) imply an ability to correctly apply and interpret the procedure. In general, studies have shown that procedural knowledge, particularly that involving mathematics, is best approached conceptually (Davis, 1984; Romberg & Carpenter, 1986).

Given that procedures commonly involve bugs, analyzing errors for mental and psychomotor procedures involves searching for and remediating them. However, as the foregoing discussion implies, the process of analyzing errors should be guided by a conceptual understanding of the procedure (Corno et al., 2002). Operationally, this means that students would examine the impact of each aspect of a mental or psychomotor procedure from the perspective of its contribution to the overall effectiveness of the procedures.

Generalizing

Generalizing, as defined in the New Taxonomy, is the process of constructing new generalizations from information that is already known or observed. This process involves inference, and these inferences go well beyond those made during the creation of a microstructure or a macrostructure. These inferences are generally considered to be somewhat inductive in nature.

Given the inferential nature of generalizing and the common understanding (or misunderstanding) of induction and deduction, it is useful to discuss the two briefly and their relationship to the process of generalizing. *Induction* is usually thought of as reasoning from the specific to the general. Holland, Holyoak, Nisbett, and Thagard (1986) postulated four rules that are the working parts of the induction process. The *specialization rule* states that if a previously generated rule does not provide accurate guidance in a specific situation, then a more specific rule should be generated. The *unusualness rule* states that if a situation has an unexpected property relative to the rule that governs the situation, a conditioned element should be added to the original rule. The *rule of large numbers* states that when generating a rule based on a sample of events or elements, the rule should be generated under the assumption that it applies to all elements in the set; however, a strength parameter should be attached to the rule proportionate with the number of events or elements that have been sampled: the more events or elements, the stronger the rule. The *regulation rule* states that if an individual has a rule of the following form: "If you want to do *X,* then you must first do *Y,*" then a rule like the following should be generated: "If you do not do *Y*, then you cannot do *X*" (p. 42).

Deduction is generally thought of as reasoning from the general to the specific. Deductive inferences are also rule based. Holland et al. (1986) identify two categories of deductive rules: *synchronic* and *diachronic*. Synchronic rules are atemporal in nature and form the basis for classification and categorization. There are two types of synchronic rules: *categorical* and *associative*. These are exemplified as follows:

1. Categorical
   a. If an object is a dog, then it is an animal.
   b. If an object is a large, slender dog with very long white and gold hair, then it is a collie.

2. Associative
   a. If an object is a dog, then activate the "cat" concept.
   b. If an object is a dog, then activate the "bone" concept.

Diachronic rules deal with basic relationships of cause-effect and temporal order. There are two types of diachronic rules: *predictor* and *effector*. These are exemplified in the following:

1. Predictor
   a. If a person annoys a dog, then the dog will growl.
   b. If a person whistles to a dog, then the dog will come to the person.

2. Effector
   a. If a dog chases you, then run away.
   b. If a dog approaches you with a wagging tail, then pet it.

Even more specific rules have been proposed by some psychologists (see Braine, 1978) as the basis for deduction. These rules are sometimes referred to as a form of mental logic. Johnson-Laird (1983; Johnson-Laird & Byrne, 1991) has developed a theory of deduction that relies on symbolic tokens.

The process of generalizing, as defined in the New Taxonomy, is neither purely inductive nor purely deductive. It is probably safe to say that no mental process is purely inductive or purely deductive. Rather, scholars assert that reasoning is often more messy and nonlinear than earlier definitions suggest (Deely, 1982; Eco, 1976, 1979, 1984; Medawar, 1967; Percy, 1975). Many philosophers have advanced the concept of *retroduction* as a more fruitful approach to understanding the nature of inferential thinking. Retroduction is the act of generating and shaping an idea based on one or more cases. Sometimes inferences made during this process are more inductive in nature; sometimes they are more deductive. Within the New

Taxonomy, generalizing is best described as a retroductive process that is oriented more toward induction than deduction but involves both during different aspects of the process. To illustrate, a student is involved in the analytic process of generalizing by constructing a new generalization about regions from three generalizations that have already been presented in class.

Critical attributes of generalizing include the following:

- Focusing on specific pieces of information or observations without making assumptions
- Looking for patterns or connections in the information
- Making a general statement that explains the patterns or connections

Specifying

As defined in the New Taxonomy, *specifying* is the process of generating new applications of a known generalization or principle. Whereas the analytic process of generalizing is more inductive, the process of specifying tends to be more deductive in nature. To illustrate, a student is involved in the analytic process of specifying by identifying a new situation or new phenomenon that is governed by Bernoulli's principle. The student has taken known principles and identified a new application previously not known to the individual.

Critical attributes of specifying include the following:

- Identifying the generalizations or principles that apply to a specific situation
- Making sure that the specific situation meets the conditions that have to be in place for those generalizations or principles to apply
- If the generalizations or principles do apply, identifying what conclusions can be drawn or what predictions can be made

Relationship to Bloom's Taxonomy

The cognitive category of analysis in the New Taxonomy incorporates elements from at least three levels of Bloom's Taxonomy. *Matching* in the New Taxonomy appears to be similar to what Bloom refers to as *analysis of relationships* within Level 4.0 (analysis) of his taxonomy. *Classification* in the New Taxonomy appears to be similar to what Bloom refers to as *identifying a set of abstract relations* within Level 5.0 (synthesis). *Analyzing errors* in the New Taxonomy as it relates to information is similar to what is referred to as *judgments in terms of internal evidence* within Level 6.0 (evaluation) of Bloom's Taxonomy. It is also similar to analysis of organizing principles within Level 4.0 (analysis) of Bloom's Taxonomy. *Generalizing* and *specifying* in the New Taxonomy appear to be similar to or embedded in many components of Levels 4, 5, and 6 of Bloom's Taxonomy. In short, *analysis* within the New Taxonomy incorporates a variety of aspects of the three highest levels of Bloom's Taxonomy.

LEVEL 4: KNOWLEDGE UTILIZATION (COGNITIVE SYSTEM)

As their name implies, knowledge utilization processes are those that individuals employ when they wish to accomplish a specific task. For example, an engineer might use knowledge of Bernoulli's principle to solve a specific problem related to lift in the design of a new type of aircraft. Specific tasks are the venue in which knowledge is rendered useful to individuals.

In the New Taxonomy, four general categories of knowledge utilization tasks have been identified: (1) decision making, (2) problem solving, (3) experimenting, and (4) investigating.

Decision Making

The process of decision making is used when an individual must select between two or more alternatives (Baron, 1982, 1985; Halpern, 1984). Metaphorically, decision making might be described as the process by which an individual answers questions such as, What is the best way to _____? or Which of these is most suitable? For example, individuals are engaged in decision making when they use their knowledge of specific locations within a city to identify the best site for a new park.

There are a number of models describing the process of decision making (see, for example, Baron, 1982, 1985; Baron & Brown, 1991; Ehrenberg, Ehrenberg, & Durfee, 1979; Halpern, 1984; Wales, Nardi, & Stager, 1986). All of these models focus on thoughtful identification of alternatives and selection among them based on sound criteria.

Problem Solving

The process of problem solving is used when an individual attempts to accomplish a goal for which an obstacle exists (Halpern, 1984; Rowe, 1985; Sternberg, 1987). Metaphorically, problem solving might be described as the process one engages in to answer questions such as, How will I overcome this obstacle? or How will I reach my goal but still meet these conditions? At its core, a defining characteristic of a problem is an obstacle or limiting condition. For example, if a young woman wishes to be at a specific location some miles from her home by a certain time and her car breaks down, she has a problem: She is attempting to accomplish a goal (i.e., to transport herself to a specific location) and an obstacle has arisen (i.e., her usual mode of transportation is not available). To address this problem effectively, she would have to use knowledge about different methods of transportation that are alternatives to taking her car (e.g., taking the bus, calling a friend) as well as options for fixing her car within the available time.

Critical attributes of the problem solving process include the following:

- Identifying obstacles to the goal
- Identifying alternative ways to accomplish the goal
- Evaluating the alternatives
- Selecting and executing the alternatives

Experimenting

Experimenting is the process of generating and testing hypotheses for the purpose of understanding some physical or psychological phenomenon. Defined as such, experimenting is rightfully thought of as central to scientific inquiry (see the selections by Bacon, Newton, Descartes, Einstein, Popper, and Kuhn in Tweney, Doherty, & Mynatt, 1981; see also Aiken, 1991; Himsworth, 1986). Metaphorically, *experimenting* might be described as the process used when answering questions such as, How can this be explained? or Based on this explanation, what can be predicted? For example, a man is involved in experimental inquiry when he generates and tests a hypothesis about the effect a new airplane wing design will have on lift and drag. It should be noted that experimenting as defined here does not employ the same rigor one would associate with scientific research. However, experimenting is based on the same underlying dynamic of hypotheses generation and testing.

Critical attributes of experimenting include the following:

- Making predictions based on known or hypothesized principles
- Designing a way to test the predictions
- Evaluating the validity of the principles based on the outcome of the test (Halpern, 1984; Ross, 1988)

Investigating

Investigating is the process of generating and testing hypotheses about past, present, or future events (Marzano, 1992; van Eemeren, Grootendorst, & Henkemans, 1996). Metaphorically, investigation may be described as the process one goes through when attempting to answer such questions as, What are the defining features of _____? or How did this happen? or Why did this happen? or What would have happened if _____? To illustrate, a student is involved in investigation when examining possible explanations for the existence of crop circles.

To some extent, the knowledge utilization process of investigation is similar to the knowledge utilization process of experimenting in that hypotheses are generated and tested. However, it differs from experimenting in that it employs different so-called rules of evidence (Abelson, 1995; Evans, Newstead, & Bryne, 1993). The rules of evidence for investigation adhere to the criteria for sound argumentation described in the discussion of analyzing errors: The evidence used to support a claim within an investigation is a well-constructed argument. However, the rules of evidence for experimenting adhere to the criteria for statistical hypotheses testing.

Critical attributes of investigating include the following:

- Identifying what is known or agreed upon regarding the phenomenon under investigation
- Identifying areas of confusion or controversy regarding the phenomenon
- Providing an answer for the confusion or controversy
- Presenting a logical argument for the proposed answer

Relationship to Bloom's Taxonomy

The overall category of *knowledge utilization* in the New Taxonomy seems most closely related to *synthesis* (Level 5.0) of Bloom's Taxonomy. Although Bloom's synthesis category does not address knowledge utilization per se, it does focus on the generation of new products and new ideas. By definition, the knowledge utilization processes of the New Taxonomy generate new products of some sort. For example, decision making generates a new awareness as to the superiority of one alternative over others, problem solving generates a new process for accomplishing a goal, and so on.

LEVEL 5: METACOGNITION

The *metacognitive system* has been described by researchers and theorists as responsible for monitoring, evaluating, and regulating the functioning of all other types of thought (Brown, 1984; Flavell, 1978; Meichenbaum & Asarnow, 1979). Taken together, these functions are sometimes referred to as responsible for executive control (Brown, 1978, 1980; Flavell, 1979, 1987; Sternberg, 1984a, 1984b, 1986a, 1986b). Within the New Taxonomy, the metacognitive system has four functions: (1) specifying goals, (2) process monitoring, (3) monitoring clarity, and (4) monitoring accuracy.

Specifying Goals

One of the primary tasks of the metacognitive system is to establish clear goals. As we see in the next section, it is the self-system that determines an individual's decision whether or not to engage in an activity. However, once the decision is made to engage, it is the metacognitive system that establishes a goal relative to that activity. In terms of the New Taxonomy, the goal-specifying function of the metacognitive system is responsible for establishing clear learning goals for specific types of knowledge. For example, it would be through the goal specification function of the metacognitive system that students would establish a specific goal or goals in terms of increasing their understanding or use of specific information presented in a mathematics class.

As part of the goal-specification process, an individual will usually identify what Hayes (1981) refers to as a clear end state—what the goal will look like when completed. This might also include the identification of milestones to be accomplished along the way. Last, it is the job of the goal specification function to develop a plan for accomplishing a given learning goal. This might include the resources that will be necessary and even timelines in which milestones and the end state will be accomplished. It is this type of thinking that has been described as strategic in nature (Paris, Lipson, & Wixson, 1983).

Process Monitoring

The process monitoring component of the metacognitive system typically monitors the effectiveness of a procedure being used in a task. For example, the metacognitive system will monitor how well the mental procedure of reading a bar graph or the physical procedure of shooting a free throw is being carried out. Quite obviously, the execution of a procedure is most effectively monitored when a goal has been set. Process monitoring also comes into play when a long-term or short-term goal has been established for information—for example, when a student has established the goal of better understanding polynomials. In this case, process monitoring addresses the extent to which that goal is being accomplished over time.

Monitoring Clarity and Accuracy

Monitoring clarity and monitoring accuracy belong to a set of functions that some researchers refer to as *dispositional* (see Amabile, 1983; Brown, 1978, 1980; Costa, 1984, 1991; Ennis, 1985, 1987a, 1987b, 1989; Flavell, 1976, 1977; Paul, 1990; Paul, 1984, 1986a; Perkins, 1984, 1985, 1986). The term *disposition* is used to indicate that monitoring clarity and monitoring accuracy are ways in which an individual is or is not disposed to approach knowledge. For example, individuals might or might not have a tendency to monitor whether they are clear or accurate about information that has been learned. It should be noted that the use of such dispositions is not automatic. Rather, individuals must consciously decide to approach given tasks with an eye toward clarity and accuracy. Perhaps for this reason, this aspect of metacognition has been associated with high intelligence or intelligent behavior (Costa, 1991).

In summary, the metacognitive system is in charge of conscious operations relative to knowledge that include goal setting, process monitoring, monitoring for clarity, and monitoring for accuracy. Salomon and Globerson (1987) refer to such thinking as being mindful:

> The individual can be expected to withhold or inhibit the evocation of a first, salient response, to examine and elaborate situational cues and underlying meanings that are relevant to the task to be accomplished, to generate or define alternative strategies, to gather information necessary for the choices to be made, to examine outcomes, to draw new connections and construct new structures and abstractions made by reflective type processes. (p. 625)

Relationship to Bloom's Taxonomy

No obvious corollary in Bloom's Taxonomy can be found to the metacognitive level as described in the New Taxonomy.

LEVEL 6: SELF-SYSTEM THINKING

The self-system consists of an interrelated arrangement of attitudes, beliefs, and emotions. It is the interaction of these attitudes, beliefs, and emotions that determines both motivation and attention. The self-system determines whether an individual will engage in or disengage in a given task; it also determines how much energy the individual will bring to the task. Once the self-system has determined what will be attended to, the functioning of all other elements of thought (i.e., the metacognitive system, the cognitive system, and the knowledge domains) are, to a certain extent, dedicated or determined. This is why the act of the self-system's selecting a task has been referred to as "crossing the Rubicon" (Garcia & Pintrich, 1993; Pintrich & Garcia, 1992).

There are four types of self-system thinking that are relevant to the New Taxonomy: (1) examining importance, (2) examining efficacy, (3) examining emotional response, and (4) examining overall motivation.

Examining Importance

One of the key determinants of whether an individual attends to a given type of knowledge is whether that individual considers the knowledge important. Obviously, if students consider the skill of reading a contour map important, they will be more likely to expend time and energy developing this mental skill.

What an individual considers to be important is probably a function of the extent to which it meets one of two conditions: it is perceived as instrumental in either satisfying a basic need or in the attainment of a personal goal. As explained by psychologists such as Maslow (1968), human beings have evolutionarily designed needs that might even exist in somewhat of a hierarchic structure. Although Maslow's hierarchy has been criticized (see Wahba & Bridwell, 1976), it provides powerful insights into human motivation. As Covington (1992) explains, "it provides a useful way of thinking about the factors that activate normal human beings" (p. 19). In Maslow's (1968) hierarchy, needs such as physical safety, food, and shelter are more basic than needs such as companionship and acceptance. If a specific knowledge component is perceived as being instrumental in meeting one or more of these needs, it will be considered important by an individual. For example, if a boy perceives that the ability to read a contour map will increase his chances of physical safety while participating in a camping trip, he will probably choose to put considerable time and energy into acquiring that mental skill.

As we've said, other than the extent to which it helps one meet basic needs, a knowledge component can be perceived as important because it is seen to be instrumental in attaining some personal goal. For example, if a young man perceives that reading a contour map will help him attain a life-long goal of becoming a forest ranger, he will probably choose to put time and energy into acquiring this skill.

The exact source of these personal goals is, to date, a bit of a mystery (Klausner, 1965). Some would assert that personal goals are functions of one's environment: Our need for acceptance propels us to construct personal goals that will increase our sense of esteem within our culture (see Bandura, 1977, 1982, 1991, 1993, 1996, 1997). Others would assert that personal goals are an outgrowth of more deeply held beliefs regarding the purpose of life. For example, philosophers such as Frankl (1967) and Buber (1958) have demonstrated that beliefs about one's ultimate purpose are a central feature of one's psychological makeup. A strong case can be made that this set of beliefs ultimately exerts control over all other elements in the self-system. To illustrate, assume that a young woman believes that her purpose in life (or one of her purposes) is to use her talents to contribute to the benefit of others.

As a consequence, she will consider those things important that contribute to this goal. She will then encode specific persons, situations, events, and the like as important or not, based on whether they are perceived as instrumental in realizing this purpose.

Regardless of psychologists' explanations regarding the ultimate source of personal goals, most agree that such goals are a primary factor in one's perception of what is important.

Examining Efficacy

Bandura's (1977, 1982, 1991, 1993, 1996, 1997) theories and research have brought the role of beliefs about efficacy to the attention of both psychologists and educators. In simple terms, beliefs about efficacy address the extent to which individuals believe they have the resources, ability, or power to change a situation. Relative to the New Taxonomy, examining efficacy would involve examining the extent to which individuals believe they have the ability, power, or necessary resources to gain competence relative to a specific knowledge component. If students believe they do not have the requisite ability, power, or resources to gain competence in a specific skill, this might greatly lessen their motivation to learn that knowledge, even though they perceive it as important.

Bandura's (1977, 1982, 1991, 1993, 1996, 1997) research indicates that a sense of efficacy is not necessarily a generalizable construct. Rather, an individual might have a strong sense of efficacy in one situation yet feel relatively powerless in another. Seligman's (1990, 1994) research also attests to the situational nature of one's sense of efficacy and underscores the importance of these beliefs. He has found that a low sense of efficacy can result in a pattern of behavior that he refers to as learned helplessness.

Examining Emotional Response

The influence of emotion in human motivation is becoming increasingly clear. Given the biology of emotions, many brain researchers assert that emotions are involved in almost every aspect of human behavior. A good case can be made for the contention that emotion exerts a controlling influence over human thought (see Katz, 1999; Pert, 1997). This case is well articulated in LeDoux's (1996) *The Emotional Brain: The Mysterious Underpinnings of Emotional Life*.

As a result of his analysis of the research on emotions, LeDoux (1996) concludes that human beings (a) have little direct control over their emotional reactions, and (b) once emotions occur, they become powerful motivators of future behavior. Relative to humans' lack of control over emotions, LeDoux notes,

> Anyone who has tried to fake an emotion, or who has been the recipient of a faked one, knows all too well the futility of the attempt. While conscious control over emotions is weak, emotions can flood consciousness. This is so because the wiring of the brain at this point in our evolutionary history is such that connections from the emotional systems to the cognitive systems are stronger than connections from the cognitive systems to the emotional systems. (p. 19)

Relative to the power of emotions once they occur, LeDoux (1996) explains,

> They chart the course of moment-to-moment action as well as set the sails toward long-term achievements. But our emotions can also get us into trouble. When fear becomes anxiety, desire gives way to greed, or annoyance turns to anger, anger to hatred, friendship to envy, love to obsession, or pleasure to addiction, our emotions start working against us. Mental health is maintained by emotional hygiene, and mental problems, to a large extent, reflect a breakdown of emotional order. Emotions can have both useful and pathological consequences. (pp. 19–20)

For LeDoux (1996), emotions are primary motivators that often outstrip an individual's system of values and beliefs relative to their influence on human behavior.

Relative to the New Taxonomy, examining emotions involves analyzing the extent to which an individual has an emotional response to a given knowledge component and the part that response plays in one's motivation. The importance of such self-analyses has received a good deal of attention in the popular press over the past three decades (see, for example, Goleman, 1995; Langer, 1989).

Examining Overall Motivation

As might be inferred from the previous discussion, an individual's motivation to initially learn or increase competence in a given knowledge component is a function of three factors: (1) perceptions of its importance, (2) perceptions of efficacy relative to learning or increasing competency in the knowledge component, and (3) one's emotional response to the knowledge component. This is depicted in Figure 3.5.

Given this set of relationships, one can operationally describe different levels of motivation. Specifically, high motivation to learn or increase

Figure 3.5   Aspects of Motivation

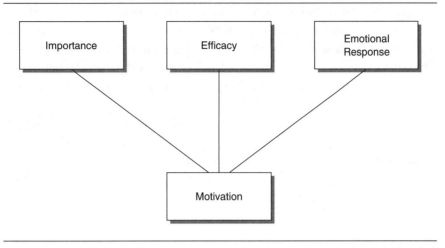

competence relative to a given knowledge component will exist under the following conditions:

1. The individual perceives the knowledge component as important.

2. The individual believes that he or she has the necessary ability, power, or resources to learn or increase his or her competence relative to the knowledge component.

3. The individual has a positive emotional response to the knowledge component.

Low motivation occurs under the following conditions:

1. The individual perceives the knowledge component to be unimportant.

2. The individual believes that he or she does not have the necessary ability, power, or resources to learn or increase his or her competence relative to the knowledge component.

3. The individual has a negative emotional response to the knowledge component.

It is important to note that these three self-system determiners are probably not equal in terms of their effect on motivation. It is likely that a perception of importance can override a perceived lack of efficacy and a negative emotional response. For example, a mother will be highly motivated to stop an oncoming car that is about to strike her young child. The mother surely does not believe that she has the physical power to stop the car (she has a low perception of efficacy in this situation), and she surely would have negative emotion associated with being struck by the car herself. However, her child's safety is such an important goal to her that it overrides or outweighs the other two elements.

In terms of the New Taxonomy, examining motivation is the process of identifying one's level of motivation to learn or increase competence in a given knowledge component and then identifying the interrelationships between one's beliefs about importance, beliefs about efficacy, and emotional response that govern one's level of motivation.

Relationship to Bloom's Taxonomy

As in the case with metacognition, the self-system component of the New Taxonomy has no obvious corollary in Bloom's Taxonomy.

REVISITING THE HIERARCHICAL NATURE OF THE NEW TAXONOMY

The hierarchical structure of the New Taxonomy is based on flow of processing. To review briefly, the self-system is the first line of processing: It determines the extent to which a student will be motivated to learn a given knowledge component. Given that the self-system has determined that the knowledge is important enough to learn, the next system to be engaged is the metacognitive system. Its task is to establish clear learning goals relative to the knowledge, then plan for and carry out those goals in as precise a manner as possible. Under the direction of the metacognitive system, the elements of the cognitive system are then employed. As we have seen, the cognitive system is responsible for processes as simple as retrieval and as complex as using the knowledge in a new context.

The three systems within the New Taxonomy are also hierarchical relative to the level of consciousness required to control their execution. Whereas cognitive processes require a certain degree of awareness and conscious thought to be executed in a controlled fashion, the metacognitive processes probably require more. Learning goals cannot be set nor can accuracy be monitored, for example, without a fair degree of mental energy. Last, examining self-system processes, such as importance and emotional response, probably represents a level of introspection and conscious thought not normally engaged in.

Consciousness of processing, which is necessary for control, is a characteristic that also discloses the hierarchic nature of the cognitive system, which consists of the first four levels of the New Taxonomy: retrieval, comprehension, analysis, and knowledge utilization. The retrieval processes, as described in the New Taxonomy, can be executed automatically; the comprehension processes require slightly more conscious thought; and analysis processes still more. Last, the utilization processes require even more conscious processing.

Given that the metacognitive processes require more conscious thought than the cognitive processes and the self-system processes require more conscious thought than the metacognitive processes, a taxonomy of six levels can be established. This is depicted in Figure 3.6.

Figure 3.6   Conscious Control and the Levels of the New Taxonomy

Conscious	Level 6:	Self-system processes
	Level 5:	Metacognitive processes
	Level 4:	Knowledge utilization processes
	Level 3:	Analysis processes
	Level 2:	Comprehension processes
Automatic	Level 1:	Retrieval processes

It is important to realize that the six levels of the New Taxonomy do not represent levels of complexity. The processes within the self-system are not more complex than the processes within the metacognitive system, and so on. This is in contrast to Bloom's Taxonomy and the Anderson et al. (2001) taxonomy, which attempt to use processing difficulty as the critical feature separating one level from the next. In addition, it is important to note that the New Taxonomy makes no claims that the components within the self- and metacognitive systems are themselves hierarchical in nature. For example, there is no necessary ordering of the processes of examining importance, efficacy, and emotional response in terms of levels of consciousness.

THE NEW TAXONOMY IN TERMS OF MENTAL OPERATIONS

The six levels of the New Taxonomy make for a rather straightforward taxonomy of mental operations that might be applied to any type of knowledge. The mental operations at each level require more conscious processing than is required at lower levels. Figure 3.7 presents an articulation of mental operations at all six levels of the New Taxonomy.

Figure 3.7   The New Taxonomy Stated as Mental Operations

Level 6: Self-System Thinking	
Examining Importance	Students identify how important the knowledge is to them and the reasoning underlying this perception.
Examining Efficacy	Students identify beliefs about their ability to improve competence or understanding relative to knowledge and the reasoning underlying this perception.
Examining Emotional Response	Students identify emotional responses to knowledge and the reasons for these responses.
Examining Motivation	Students identify their overall level of motivation to improve competence or understanding relative to knowledge and the reasons for this level of motivation.

Level 5: Metacognition	
Specifying Goals	Students establish a goal relative to the knowledge and a plan for accomplishing the goal.
Process Monitoring	Students monitor the execution of specific goals as they relate to the knowledge.
Monitoring Clarity	Students determine the extent to which they have clarity about the knowledge.
Monitoring Accuracy	Students determine the extent to which they are accurate about the knowledge.

Level 4: Knowledge Utilization	
Decision Making	Students use the knowledge to make decisions or make decisions about the knowledge.
Problem Solving	Students use the knowledge to solve problems or solve problems about the knowledge.
Experimenting	Students use the knowledge to generate and test hypotheses or generate and test hypotheses about the knowledge.
Investigating	Students use the knowledge to conduct investigations or conduct investigations about the knowledge.

Level 3: Analysis	
Matching	Students identify important similarities and differences between knowledge components.
Classifying	Students identify superordinate and subordinate categories related to the knowledge.
Analyzing Errors	Students identify errors in the presentation or use of the knowledge.
Generalizing	Students construct new generalizations or principles based on the knowledge.
Specifying	Students identify specific applications or logical consequences of the knowledge.

Level 2: Comprehension	
Integrating	Students identify the basic structure of knowledge and the critical as opposed to noncritical characteristics.
Symbolizing	Students construct an accurate symbolic representation of the knowledge, differentiating critical and noncritical components.

Level 1: Retrieval	
Recognizing	Students recognize features of information but do not necessarily understand the structure of the knowledge or differentiate critical from noncritical components.
Recalling	Students produce features of information but do not necessarily understand the structure of the knowledge or differentiate critical from noncritical components.
Executing	Students perform a procedure without significant error but do not necessarily understand how and why the procedure works.

These six levels of processing interact with the three knowledge domains described in Chapter 2. The next chapter details the specifics of these interactions.

SUMMARY

This chapter has described the six levels of the New Taxonomy within the context of three systems of thought—cognitive, metacognitive, and self-system. The cognitive system includes processes that address retrieval, comprehension, analysis, and knowledge utilization. The metacognitive system includes processes that address specifying goals, process monitoring, and disposition monitoring. The self-system includes processing dedicated to examining importance, examining efficacy, and examining emotional response. It is the interaction of these elements that dictates one's motivation and attention.

CHAPTER FOUR

The New Taxonomy and the Three Knowledge Domains

As described in previous chapters, knowledge within any subject area can be organized into the domains of information, mental processes, and psychomotor processes. The six levels of the New Taxonomy interact in different ways with these three knowledge domains. In this chapter, we discuss each of the three knowledge domains in light of the six levels of the New Taxonomy. Before doing so, however, it is worth underscoring the difference between this approach and that taken in Bloom's Taxonomy.

Bloom's Taxonomy addressed the differences in types of knowledge at the first level only. There, Bloom distinguished between terms versus details versus generalizations and so on. However, these distinctions were not carried through to the other five levels of the taxonomy. No discussion was provided as to how Bloom's process of evaluation is different for details than it is for generalizations, for instance.

In contrast, as articulated in this chapter, the New Taxonomy explicitly defines the manner in which each of its six levels interacts with the three knowledge domains. In effect the New Taxonomy is two-dimensional in nature: One dimension is the six levels of the taxonomy, the other is the three knowledge domains. This is depicted in Figure 4.1.

LEVEL 1: RETRIEVAL

Retrieval involves the simple recognition, recall, or execution of knowledge. There is no expectation that the student will know the knowledge in depth, be able to identify the basic structure of the knowledge (or its critical versus noncritical elements), or use it to accomplish complex goals. These are all expectations for higher levels of the New Taxonomy. As described previously,

Figure 4.1   The New Taxonomy

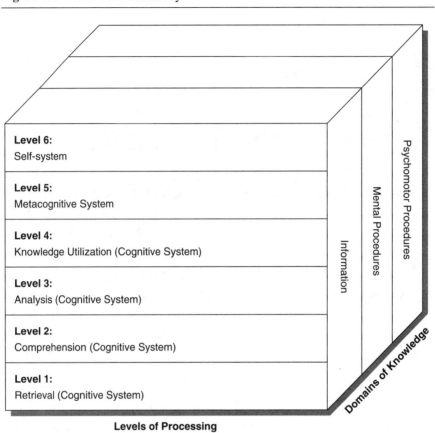

the information domain involves declarative knowledge only; declarative knowledge can be recognized or recalled but not executed. The domains of mental and psychomotor procedures involve procedural knowledge, and knowledge in these two domains can be recognized, recalled, and executed. Although the processes of recognizing, recalling, and executing are highly related, we consider them separately since they imply different types of tasks that might be presented to students.

Recognizing

Tasks that relate to the retrieval process of recognizing across the three knowledge domains are presented in Figure 4.2.

Figure 4.2   Recognizing Tasks

Information	
Details	When presented with statements about specific details, the student validates their accuracy.
Organizing Ideas	When presented with statements about organizing ideas, the student validates their accuracy.
Mental Procedures	
Skills	When presented with statements about a mental skill, the student validates their accuracy.
Processes	When presented with statements about a mental process, the student validates their accuracy.
Psychomotor Procedures	
Skills	When presented with statements about a psychomotor skill, the student validates their accuracy.
Processes	When presented with statements about a psychomotor process, the student validates their accuracy.

1. Recognizing Information

To demonstrate recognition of simple details within the domain of information, students must identify accurate statements regarding terms, facts, and time sequences; however, they might not be able to produce such statements. The following question would elicit recognition about a specific fact:

Jean Valjean was first sentenced to prison for which of the following?

   a. Stealing a loaf of bread

   b. Stealing the Bishop's candlesticks

   c. Not paying taxes on a cow he bought

   d. Refusing to join the French army

Demonstrating recognition of organizing ideas involves identifying accurate statements about generalizations and principles. The following question would elicit recognition of an organizing idea:

Which of the following is least likely to be linked to adolescent suicide?

   a. Depression

   b. Mental illness

   c. Drug and alcohol abuse

   d. Diabetes

To correctly answer this item, a student must understand a principle about potential causes of adolescent suicide and the relative probability of those causes.

2. Recognizing Mental Procedures

Recognizing as it relates to mental skills involves validating statements regarding a mental skill. For example, the following item would elicit recognition regarding a mental skill:

Which of the following is probably *least* likely to be the *first* step you would take when presented with a map you had never seen before?

    a. Look at the map legend

    b. Start locating specific places

    c. Identify the general territory the map includes

    d. Look at the title of the map

A student demonstrates recognition of the mental process of using a specific word-processing software program (e.g. Microsoft Word) by validating the accuracy of statements about the process. The following task would elicit this type of thinking:

Place a T next to the statements that are true about using Microsoft Word and F next to statements that are false.

    _____ When a file is open, you can rename it as many times as you wish.

    _____ You must use the same font type throughout a document, but you can change the font size.

    _____ You can indent at more than one level in a document.

3. Recognizing Psychomotor Procedures

Recognizing as it relates to psychomotor procedures involves validating the accuracy of statements about psychomotor skills and processes. The following questions would elicit this type of thinking:

Psychomotor Skill: Which of the following statements are true about stretching the hamstring muscle?

    _____ a. It is best to stretch the muscle to the point at which you begin to feel pain.

    _____ b. When a hamstring muscle has been pulled, you should rest it until you feel no tightness.

    _____ c. When stretching the hamstring, you should use slow gradual movements.

Psychomotor Process: Which of the following statements are true about playing person-to-person defense in basketball?

_____ a. The proper body position is to keep your feet close together so that you can move in any direction.

_____ b. You should have one of your hands up high and one down low.

_____ c. You should never try to interrupt your opponent's dribble.

Recalling

Recalling involves generating as opposed to simply recognizing information. Figure 4.3 presents recalling tasks across the three domains of knowledge.

Figure 4.3   Recalling Tasks

Information	
Details	When asked about specific details, the student produces related information.
Organizing Ideas	When presented with a principle or generalization, the student produces related information.
Mental Procedures	
Skills	When asked, the student describes the general nature and purpose of a mental skill.
Processes	When asked, the student describes the general nature and purpose of a mental process.
Psychomotor Procedures	
Skills	When asked, the student describes the general nature and purpose of a psychomotor skill.
Processes	When asked, the student describes the general nature and purpose of a psychomotor process.

1. Recalling Information

To demonstrate recall of simple details within the domain of information, students must produce accurate but not necessarily critical information about terms, facts, and time sequences.

The following question would elicit recall about a specific vocabulary term:

We have been studying the term *synapse*. Briefly explain what it means.

Demonstrating knowledge recall for organizing ideas within the domain of information involves articulating examples of a generalization or a principle.

For example, a student demonstrates recall of an organizing idea by producing examples of generalizations about the origin of life. The following question would elicit this type of thinking:

We have been studying examples of the generalization that "all life comes from life and produces its own kind of living organism." Identify two examples of this that we have studied.

The following question would elicit knowledge recall relative to a principle:

Coulomb's law of electrostatic attraction states that "the force of attraction or repulsion between two charged bodies is directly proportional to the product of the charges, and inversely proportional to the square of the distance between them." Describe two consequences we have studied about this law.

It is important to note that both foregoing questions make mention of the fact that examples or applications have already been addressed (i.e., Identify two examples . . . we have studied). This is because recall, by definition, involves information that is known, not information newly generated. Asking students to generate new examples of a generalization or principle is better described as analysis (Level 3 of the New Taxonomy).

2. Recalling Mental Procedures

Knowledge recall relative to a mental skill involves generating basic information about a mental skill. For example, a student would be demonstrating knowledge recall relative to the mental skill of reading a contour map by describing the skill. The following task would elicit this type of thinking:

Describe some of the things you would do when reading a new contour map.

A student demonstrates recall of the mental process of using Microsoft Word by explaining but not actually executing aspects of the process. The following question would elicit this type of thinking:

Explain the steps you would take to rename an open file.

3. Recalling Psychomotor Procedures

Knowledge recall relative to psychomotor procedures involves generating basic information about a psychomotor skill or process. For example, the following tasks would elicit recall regarding the psychomotor skill of stretching the hamstring muscle and the psychomotor process of playing person-to-person defense in basketball, respectively:

Psychomotor Skill: We have been examining the proper technique for stretching the hamstrings. What are situations in which it is useful to use this technique? Describe the basic steps involved.

Psychomotor Process: Describe the proper technique for playing person-to-person defense.

Executing

Figure 4.4 presents executing tasks across the three domains of knowledge.

Figure 4.4   Executing Tasks

Information	
Details	Not applicable
Organizing Ideas	Not applicable
Mental Procedures	
Skills	When asked, the student performs the mental skill without significant error.
Processes	When asked, the student performs the mental process without significant error.
Psychomotor Procedures	
Skills	When asked, the student performs the psychomotor skill without significant error.
Processes	When asked, the student performs the psychomotor process without significant error.

As depicted in Figure 4.4, the retrieval process of executing does not apply to information. However, the ultimate indicator of a student's knowledge of a mental or psychomotor procedure is whether he or she can perform or execute it without significant error. As described previously, executing does not imply that students have an understanding of how or why a procedure works, only that they can perform it.

Tasks for mental and psychomotor procedures follow the same general pattern as exemplified by the following:

1. Executing Mental Procedures

Mental Skill: You have been given a contour map of the area surrounding our school. Describe some of the information it provides about this area.

Mental Process: On your desk you will find a copy of a letter. Using the program Microsoft Word, type this letter, save it, and print it out on letterhead paper.

2. Executing Psychomotor Procedures

Psychomotor Skill: Demonstrate the proper method of stretching the hamstring muscles.

Psychomotor Process: Select a partner and play a game of one-on-one basketball to five goals. Demonstrate proper person-to-person defense while doing so.

LEVEL 2: COMPREHENSION

The comprehension processes require more of students than do the knowledge retrieval processes. Where knowledge retrieval involves recognition, recall, or execution of knowledge as learned, comprehension involves the integration and symbolic representation of the more important versus the less important aspects of that knowledge. It is much more generative in nature in that it typically involves the altering of knowledge that has been deposited in working memory. There are two related comprehension processes: integrating and symbolizing.

Integrating

Integrating involves reducing knowledge down to its key parts. As described previously, in technical terms, integrating involves creating a macrostructure for knowledge—a parsimonious accounting of the key elements of the knowledge usually at a more general level than originally experienced. Figure 4.5 lists tasks for knowledge integration across the three knowledge domains.

Figure 4.5   Integrating Tasks

Information	
Details	When asked, the student identifies the essential versus nonessential elements of specific details.
Organizing Ideas	When asked, the student identifies the defining characteristics of a generalization or principle.
Mental Procedures	
Skills	When asked, the student describes the logic of the steps involved in a mental skill.
Processes	When asked, the student describes the logic of the major aspects of a mental process.
Psychomotor Procedures	
Skills	When asked, the student describes the logic of the steps involved in a psychomotor skill.
Processes	When asked, the student describes the logic of the major aspects of a psychomotor process.

1. Integrating Information

In some situations, integrating can be applied to details. Since integrating involves identifying essential versus nonessential elements, a set of details must have a fairly complex structure to be amenable to integrating. For example, the events occurring at the Alamo might be complex enough to warrant the comprehension process of integrating. At the level of recall, students would be expected to remember the general nature of these events only. At the level of integrating, however, students would be expected to identify those events that were critical to the final outcome versus those that were not. The following task would elicit knowledge integration relative to this event:

Identify those events that happened at the Alamo that were critical to its outcome versus those that were not.

Given their inherent complexity, organizing ideas are highly amenable to integrating. However, the process of integrating is somewhat different for principles than it is for generalizations. Relative to principles, the process results in an understanding of relationships between the variables that are addressed in the principle. As described in Chapter 2, relationships between variables can take many forms. For example, the increase in one variable is associated with an increase in the other, or an increase in one variable is associated with a decrease in the other. To demonstrate integration of a principle a student must describe the variables associated with the principle and the precise nature of their relationship. For example, a student would demonstrate integration of a principle by identifying and describing the relationship between the number of lemmings in an Arctic habitat and the number of caribou in the same habitat or by describing the relationship between the amount of carbonate dissolved in the water of a river and the number of clams in that river. The following tasks would elicit the process of integrating as they relate to these examples:

1. There is a relationship between the number of lemmings in the Arctic habitat and the number of caribou in the same habitat. Describe that relationship. Be careful to include all the major factors that affect this relationship.

2. Describe the relationship between the number of clams in a river and the amount of carbonate dissolved in the water. What are some of the factors affecting this relationship, and how do they affect it?

It is important to note that these tasks should require students to go beyond recalling what was presented in class in that information that has been taught is to be organized and stated in new ways.

Integrating as it relates to generalizations involves the identification of critical versus noncritical attributes of the generalization. Recall from Chapter 2 that a generalization is a statement about a class of persons, places, things, events, or abstractions. Integrating as it relates to generalizations, then, involves identifying the defining characteristics of a class as opposed to related, but not defining, characteristics. For example, a student would demonstrate integration of a generalization about golden retrievers by identifying characteristics that define this class of canine as opposed to those that are associated with the category but do not define it. Again, an integration task should require more than recalling what was presented in class. The following question would elicit this type of integrating:

What are the defining features of mutualism as opposed to those features that are associated with this type of relationship but are not defining characteristics?

2. Integrating Mental Procedures

Integrating relative to a mental skill or process involves identifying and articulating the various steps of that skill or process as well as the order of those steps and the logic of that order. It involves more than the recall of the steps in that it requires the student to comment on the rationale underlying the process. The following question would elicit integrating relative to the mental skill of reading a bar graph:

Describe the steps you go through when you read a bar graph. Explain whether those steps must be performed in any specific order.

The following question would elicit integrating relative to the mental process of using WordPerfect:

Describe the steps you must go through to write a letter, save it, and print it out using WordPerfect. How do the various parts of this process relate to one another?

3. Integrating Psychomotor Procedures

Integrating applies to psychomotor skills and processes in the same way it applies to mental skills and processes. A student demonstrates integrating relative to the psychomotor skill of making a backhand shot in tennis by describing the component parts of the action and their interrelationship. A student demonstrates integrating relative to the process of returning a serve in tennis by describing the skills and strategies involved and their interactions. The following questions would elicit this type of thinking:

Describe the best way to make a backhand shot. What are the critical elements in hitting a good backhand?

Explain the skills and strategies involved in returning a serve. How do these skills and strategies interact with one another?

Symbolizing

The comprehension process of symbolizing involves depicting knowledge in some type of nonlinguistic or abstract form. Figure 4.6 lists tasks for the comprehension process of symbolizing across the three knowledge domains.

Figure 4.6   Symbolizing Tasks

Information	
Details	When asked, the student accurately represents the major aspects of details in nonlinguistic or abstract form.
Organizing Ideas	When asked, the student accurately represents the major components of a generalization or principle and their relationship in nonlinguistic or abstract form.
Mental Procedures	
Skills	When asked, the student accurately represents the component parts of a mental skill in nonlinguistic or abstract form.
Processes	When asked, the student accurately represents the component parts of a mental process in nonlinguistic or abstract form.
Psychomotor Procedures	
Skills	When asked, the student accurately represents the component parts of a psychomotor skill in nonlinguistic or abstract form.
Processes	When asked, the student accurately represents the component parts of a psychomotor process in nonlinguistic or abstract form.

It is important to note that each of the descriptions in Figure 4.6 emphasizes the need for accuracy in the student's representation. Indeed, as described in Chapter 3, the process of symbolizing assumes an accurate integration of knowledge. Consequently, to demonstrate symbolizing knowledge, a student would necessarily have integrated that knowledge.

1. Symbolizing Information

Symbolizing details can be elicited from students by fairly straightforward requests. For example, if a teacher wished to determine students' ability to symbolize their understanding of the term *heredity,* he or she might give a direction such as the following:

> In this unit we have used the term *heredity.* Illustrate what you consider to be the important aspect of the term using a graphic representation or a pictograph.

If a teacher wished to elicit the process of symbolizing about a specific event, he or she might make the following request of students:

> Represent the key events that occurred when Iraq invaded Kuwait in 1989.

Symbolizing details can be done in a wide variety of ways. For example, one student might choose to represent the key information about heredity as a graphic organizer, while another might choose to represent it as a pictograph, and still another as a picture.

The appropriate forms of symbolizing are somewhat more limited for organizing ideas. Specifically, as described in Chapter 3, generalizations lend themselves to certain types of representations and not others. One of the most common is that depicted in Figure 4.7 for a representation of the generalization that "dictators rise to power when countries are weak by promising them strength."

The following task would elicit symbolizing relative to this generalization:

> Design a graph that represents the generalization that "dictators rise to power when countries are weak by promising them strength."

Given that principles describe relationships between variables, they are commonly symbolized by graphs. For example, Figure 4.8 contains a graphic representation a student might construct to symbolize the relationship between the number of lemmings in an Arctic habitat and the number of caribou in the same habitat.

The following question would elicit this type of thinking:

> Create a graph that represents the relationship between the number of lemmings in an Arctic habitat and the number of caribou in the same habitat.

2. Symbolizing Mental and Psychomotor Procedures

Relative to both mental and psychomotor procedures, symbolizing commonly involves the construction of a diagram or flow chart that depicts the flow of activity. For example, Figure 4.9 contains a diagrammatic representation a student might generate for the skill of reading a bar graph.

Figure 4.7   Representation for Generalization

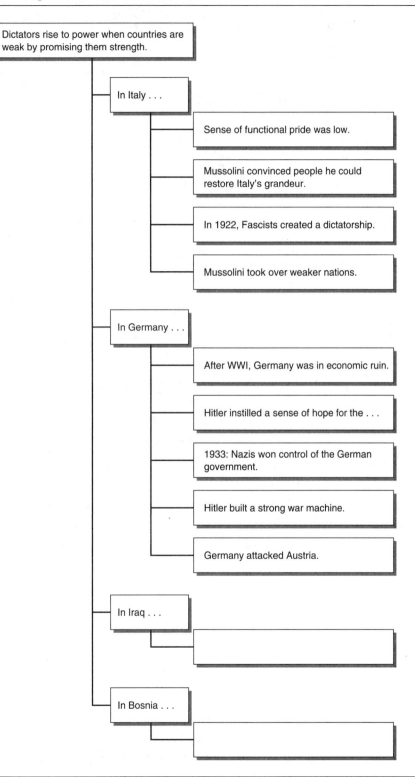

Figure 4.8   Representation for Principle

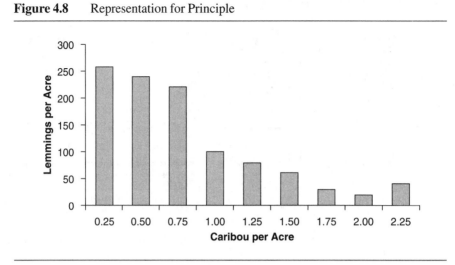

Figure 4.9   Representation for Skill

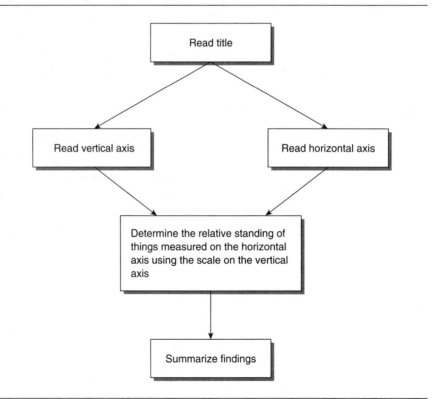

The following tasks would elicit symbolizing as it relates to mental and psychomotor procedures:

Mental skill: Draw a diagram that represents the thinking you go through when you read a bar graph.

Mental process: Construct a diagram that represents that process of writing, storing, and printing a letter using WordPerfect.

Psychomotor skill: Draw a diagram that represents the action involved in making a backhand stroke in tennis.

Psychomotor process: Draw a diagram that represents what you do when you return a serve in tennis.

LEVEL 3: ANALYSIS

As described in Chapter 2, the analysis processes all involve examining knowledge in fine detail and, as a result, generating new conclusions. There are five analysis processes: (1) matching, (2) classifying, (3) analyzing errors, (4) generalizing, and (5) specifying.

Matching

Matching involves identifying similarities and differences. Figure 4.10 lists matching tasks across the three knowledge domains.

Figure 4.10 Matching Tasks

Information	
Details	When asked, the student identifies how specific details are similar and different.
Organizing Ideas	When asked, the student identifies how generalizations or principles are similar and different.
Mental Procedures	
Skills	When asked, the student identifies how mental skills are similar and different.
Processes	When asked, the student identifies how mental processes are similar and different.
Psychomotor Procedures	
Skills	When asked, the student identifies how psychomotor skills are similar and different.
Processes	When asked, the student identifies how psychomotor processes are similar and different.

1. Matching Information

As it relates to details, matching involves identifying the manner in which a term, fact, or time sequence is similar to, yet different from, related structures. For example, a student demonstrates the ability to match knowledge of the events of the Battle of Gettysburg by determining how it is similar to and different from other battles. The following task would elicit this type of thinking:

Describe how the Battle of Gettysburg is similar to and different from the Battle of Atlanta.

Matching can involve more than two examples of a specific type of knowledge. For example, a student demonstrates the ability to match by organizing individuals from history into two or more groups based on their similarities. The following task would elicit this type of matching:

We have been studying a number of individuals who were important historically for one reason or another. Organize these individuals into two or more groups and explain how the individuals within each group are similar. Also explain how the individuals are different from group to group:

Alexander Graham Bell

Galileo

George Washington Carver

Louis Pasteur

Amelia Earhart

Sally Ride

John Glenn

Henry Ford

Eric the Red

Ferdinand Magellan

Jacques Cartier

Martin Luther King, Jr.

Relative to organizing ideas, matching involves identifying how one principle or generalization is similar to and different from other principles or generalizations. The following question would elicit the process of matching relative to two principles:

Below are two sets of variables found in nature. Identify the principle underlying each and explain how these principles are similar and different.

Set 1:

    a. The amount of vegetation per square yard of soil

    b. The amount of available nitrate salts in the same area of soil

Set 2:

    a. Crop yield per acre of farmland cultivated in Illinois

    b. Amount of soil nutrients per acre of farmland

Given the structure of principles, the main emphasis in matching them is on describing the similarities and differences between the relationships of the variables addressed in the principles. Generalizations, however, involve statements about classes of persons, places, living and nonliving things, events, and abstractions. Consequently, the process of matching generalizations is one of determining how the defining characteristics of two or more categories are similar and different. The following task would elicit this type of thinking:

We have been studying various characteristics of democratic politicians versus republican politicians. Identify how they are similar and different in specific characteristics.

2. Matching Mental and Psychomotor Procedures

Matching, as it relates to mental skills, involves identifying how two or more skills are similar and different in terms of the steps they involve. For example, a student would demonstrate the process of matching by articulating how reading a political map is similar to and different from reading a contour map. The following task would elicit this type of thinking:

Describe how reading a political map is similar to and different from reading a contour map.

Similarly, matching as it relates to mental processes involves identifying similarities and differences between the components of two or more processes. For example, a student demonstrates matching relative to the process of writing a poem by describing how this process is similar to and different from that of writing a story. The following task would elicit this type of thinking in students:

Describe how the process of writing a poem is similar to and different from that of writing a story.

Last, matching, as it relates to psychomotor skills and processes, is identical to matching as it relates to mental skills and procedures. Examples of questions that would elicit matching relative to psychomotor procedures follow:

Psychomotor Skills: Describe how the process of hitting a backhand shot in tennis is similar to and different from the process of hitting a forehand shot.

Psychomotor Processes: Describe how the process of returning a serve is similar to and different from the process of charging the net in tennis.

Classifying

Classifying as defined in the New Taxonomy goes beyond organizing items into groups or categories. That is a function of matching. Rather, classifying involves identifying the superordinate categories particular knowledge belongs to as well as subordinate categories into which the knowledge can be organized. Figure 4.11 lists classifying tasks across the three knowledge domains.

Figure 4.11   Classifying Tasks

Information	
Details	When asked, the student identifies the superordinate category to which specific details belong.
Organizing Ideas	When asked, the student identifies superordinate and subordinate categories for a generalization or principle.
Mental Procedures	
Skills	When asked, the student identifies superordinate categories for a mental skill.
Processes	When asked, the student identifies superordinate and subordinate categories for a mental process.
Psychomotor Procedures	
Skills	When asked, the student identifies superordinate categories for a psychomotor skill.
Processes	When asked, the student identifies superordinate and subordinate categories for a psychomotor process.

1. Classifying Information

In terms of details, classifying involves the identification of superordinate categories only. For example, a student demonstrates the ability to classify a detail by identifying a general class or category of events to which the Battle of Gettysburg might belong. The following question would elicit this type of thinking:

To what general category of events would you assign the Battle of Gettysburg? Explain why you think this event falls into this category.

Since details by definition are quite specific, it is unlikely that they could be organized into subordinate classes or categories.

Classifying organizing ideas involves identifying superordinate categories as well as subordinate categories that are associated with a generalization or principle. To illustrate, a student would demonstrate classification of Bernoulli's principle by identifying a more general category of principles or theory to which it belongs. The following task would elicit this type of thinking:

We have been studying Bernoulli's principle. Identify a class of principles or a general theory to which it belongs. Explain the features of Bernoulli's principle that make it a member of the category you have identified.

The following task would elicit the identification of categories subordinate to Bernoulli's principle:

Bernoulli's principle has many applications. Describe two or more categories of these applications.

2. Classifying Mental Procedures

In terms of mental skills, classifying involves identifying superordinate categories only. Like details, skills are generally too specific to involve subordinate categories. For example, a student demonstrates classification of the skill of reading a bar graph by identifying a more general category of skill to which it belongs. The following questions would elicit this type of thinking:

To what category of skills does reading a bar graph belong? Explain why.

What are the characteristics of reading a bar graph that make you say it belongs to this category?

Classification of mental processes can involve the identification of superordinate and subordinate categories. The following questions would elicit this type of thinking:

To what general category of processes does writing belong? What are the characteristics of writing that make it belong to this category?

Identify some types of writing that require slight differences in the steps you would use. How are these types of writing similar to, yet different from, each other?

3. Classifying Psychomotor Procedures

Classification of psychomotor skills is similar to classifying mental skills. The following question would elicit classification of the psychomotor skill of stretching the hamstring muscles:

> We have been studying how to properly stretch the hamstring muscles. To what general category of activity does this skill belong? Explain what there is about stretching the hamstring muscle that makes you say it belongs to this category?

Classification of psychomotor processes is analogous to classification of mental processes. The following questions would elicit classification of the psychomotor process of warming up:

> To what general category of processes does warming up belong? Explain why it belongs to this category.

> What are some specific types of warming up? Explain how these types are similar and different.

Analyzing Errors

Analyzing errors involves identifying factual or logical errors in knowledge or processing errors in the execution of knowledge. As depicted in Figure 4.12, the skill of analyzing errors plays out somewhat differently

Figure 4.12   Analyzing Errors Tasks

Information	
Details	When asked, the student determines the reasonableness or accuracy of information regarding specific details.
Organizing Ideas	When asked, the student determines the reasonableness or accuracy of examples of a generalization or new applications of a principle.
Mental Procedures	
Skills	When asked, the student identifies errors made during the execution of a mental skill.
Processes	When asked, the student identifies errors made during the execution of a mental process.
Psychomotor Procedures	
Skills	When asked, the student identifies errors made during the execution of a psychomotor skill.
Processes	When asked, the student identifies errors made during the execution of a psychomotor process.

across the different knowledge domains. However, one characteristic common to all applications of analyzing errors is that they involve information that is false or inaccurate.

1. Analyzing Errors With Information

In terms of details, analyzing errors involves determining the extent to which information is reasonable, given what the students already know about the topic. For example, students demonstrate analyzing errors when they determine the plausibility of new information they are reading about the Battle of the Little Big Horn, based on what they already know about that incident. The following question would elicit analyzing errors in this situation:

> The attached article contains information about the Battle of the Little Big Horn that we have not addressed in class. Explain which information seems reasonable and why and which information does not seem reasonable and why.

Analyzing errors relative to organizing ideas involves determining whether the examples of a generalization or applications of a principle are logical. For example, a student demonstrates analyzing errors relative to known principles about the sun and its relationship to earth by identifying false conclusions someone might infer and explains why they are false. The following task would elicit this type of thinking:

> John knows that you are most likely to get sunburned if you are out in the sun between 11:00 a.m. and 1:00 p.m. He asks six of his friends why this is so. They each give him a different answer. Identify which of the answers are wrong and explain the errors made in each case:
>
> Answer 1: We are slightly closer to the sun at noon than in the morning or afternoon.
>
> Answer 2: More "burn" will be produced by the noon sun than by the morning or afternoon sun.
>
> Answer 3: When the sun's rays fall straight down (directly) on a surface, more energy is received than when they fall indirectly on the surface.
>
> Answer 4: When the sun is directly overhead, its rays pass through less atmosphere than when it is lower in the sky.
>
> Answer 5: The air is usually warmer at noon than at any other time of the day.
>
> Answer 6: The ultraviolet rays of sunlight are mainly responsible for sunburn.

A special form of analyzing errors occurs when a student examines the reasonableness of a newly generated generalization. In such cases, the student not only considers the accuracy of the information presented but also the extent to which the generalization is presented with the proper support (e.g., grounds, warrants, backing, and qualifiers, as described in Chapter 3). The following task elicits this type of thinking:

> The following article presents a case for the generalization that global warming is not occurring. Examine and discuss the accuracy of the writer's facts and the logic he uses to support his conclusions.

2. Analyzing Errors With Mental Procedures

In terms of mental skills and processes, analyzing errors involves identifying errors that someone is making or has made while executing the process. For example, a student demonstrates analyzing errors relative to the mental skill of adding fractions by identifying and describing mistakes that someone has made in carrying out this procedure. The following task would elicit this type of thinking:

> John has added two-thirds and three-fourths and come up with five-sevenths. Describe possible errors he has made in his computation.

The following task would elicit analyzing errors relative to the mental process of using the word-processing software WordPerfect:

> Robert plans to perform the following steps to write a composition using WordPerfect. Identify what will go wrong if he carries out the following steps exactly as stated:
>
> 1. When he gets into WordPerfect, he will begin by clicking on the CENTER command on the bar at the top of the page.
> 2. He will type in his three-paragraph composition.
> 3. When he is done, he will click on the small x in the upper-right-hand corner of the screen.
> 4. The next day he will reopen WordPerfect and print out his composition.

3. Analyzing Errors With Psychomotor Procedures

Analyzing errors for psychomotor procedures is basically identical to analyzing errors for mental procedures. It involves the identification of errors someone has made or is making while carrying out the skill or process. The following task would elicit analyzing errors relative to a psychomotor skill:

I am going to demonstrate the backhand stroke in tennis, but I'm going to make some mistakes. Describe what I am doing incorrectly and the effects these errors will have.

The following task would elicit analyzing errors relative to a psychomotor process:

Shortly you will see a brief videotape of a woman returning serves in tennis. Describe the errors she is making and the effects they are having.

Generalizing

The analysis skill of generalizing involves inferring new generalizations and principles from information that is known. Figure 4.13 lists generalizing tasks across the three knowledge domains.

Figure 4.13 Generalizing Tasks

Information	
Details	When asked, the student constructs and defends new generalizations and principles based on known details.
Organizing Ideas	When asked, the student constructs and defends new generalizations and principles based on known generalizations or principles.
Mental Procedures	
Skills	When asked, the student constructs and defends new generalizations and principles based on information about specific mental skills.
Processes	When asked, the student constructs and defends new generalizations and principles based on information about specific mental processes.
Psychomotor Procedures	
Skills	When asked, the student constructs and defends new generalizations and principles based on information about specific psychomotor skills.
Processes	When asked, the student constructs and defends new generalizations and principles based on information about specific psychomotor processes.

1. Generalizing With Information

As it relates to details, generalizing involves inferring generalizations and principles from such specific elements as terms, facts, or events. For example, a student demonstrates the analytic skill of generalizing relative to a detail by constructing a generalization or principle about the nature of political assassinations based on specific events that have been addressed in class. The following question would elicit this type of thinking:

> We have been studying a number of political assassinations that have occurred. Based on these examples, what generalizations can you make about political assassinations? Be sure to provide evidence for your conclusions.

Generalizing is a fairly sophisticated skill as it relates to organizing ideas. It involves the articulation of new generalizations and principles based on known generalizations and principles. For example, a student demonstrates generalizing as it relates to organizing ideas by constructing a new conclusion about life on earth based on a set of related principles and generalizations. The following question would elicit this type of thinking:

> Here follow a set of statements we have been studying about life on earth. What are some conclusions you might come to that are supported by these generalizations? Explain your reasoning.
>
> - There have been profound changes in the climate over the earth.
> - Coordination and integration of action is generally slower in plants than in animals.
> - There is an increasing complexity of structure and function from lower to higher forms of life.
> - All life comes from life and produces its own kind of living organism.
> - Light is a limiting factor of life.

2. Generalizing With Mental Procedures

Generalizing, as it relates to mental skills, involves constructing and defending conclusions about a set of skills. For example, students demonstrate generalizing when they generate a new conclusion about reading charts and graphs in general from their understanding of the skills involved in reading particular types of charts and graphs. The following question would elicit this type of thinking:

> What generalization or conclusion can you infer about reading charts and graphs in general from your understanding of the steps involved in reading the following types of charts and graphs: bar graphs, pie charts, histograms, and line graphs? What specific information did you use to infer your conclusion, and how does that information support your conclusion?

Generalizing as it relates to mental processes is similar to generalization as it relates to skills. Students infer new conclusions based on their understanding of two or more processes. The following question would elicit this type of thinking:

What conclusions can you infer about the process of composing in general based on your understanding of the following: the process of painting a picture, the process of writing a song, the process of writing a story? What specific information did you use to generate this new conclusion?

3. Generalizing With Psychomotor Procedures

Psychomotor procedures follow the same pattern as mental procedures. The following question would elicit generalizing as it relates to psychomotor skills:

What general conclusion can you infer about batting, based on your understanding of the following skills?

- Hitting a curve ball
- Hitting a fast ball
- Hitting a knuckle ball
- Hitting a slider

The following question would elicit generalization relative to psychomotor processes:

What general conclusion can you infer about defensive play, based on your understanding of the following?

- Playing person-to-person defense in basketball
- Defending a receiver in football
- Defending against a strong serve in tennis

Specifying

The analysis skill of specifying involves making and defending predictions about what might happen or what will necessarily happen in a given situation. Figure 4.14 lists tasks for specifying across the three knowledge domains.

1. Specifying With Information

As depicted in Figure 4.14, specifying does not apply to details, because details are inherently too specific to involve rules from which predictions can be made. On the other hand, specifying is a natural type of thinking relative to organizing ideas that, by definition, are rule based.

Figure 4.14   Specifying Tasks

Information	
Details	Not applicable
Organizing Ideas	When asked, the student identifies characteristics that might be true or must be true under certain conditions relative to a given generalization or principle.
Mental Procedures	
Skills	When asked, the student makes and defends inferences about what might happen or must happen under certain conditions relative to a mental skill.
Processes	When asked, the student makes and defends inferences about what might happen or must happen under certain conditions relative to a mental process.
Psychomotor Procedures	
Skills	When asked, the student makes and defends inferences about what might happen or must happen under certain conditions relative to a psychomotor skill.
Processes	When asked, the student makes and defends inferences about what might happen or must happen under certain conditions relative to a psychomotor process.

Specifying, as it relates to generalizations, involves identifying what might be or must be true about a specific item based on an understanding of the class or category to which that item belongs. For example, a student demonstrates knowledge specification by generating and defending statements about what must be true about a specific type of bear given his or her knowledge of bears in general. The following question would elicit this type of thinking:

A new species of bear has been discovered in Alaska. Given that it is a type of Alaskan bear, what are some characteristics it must possess and some characteristics it might possess? On what basis did you identify those characteristics that it must possess versus those characteristics it might possess?

Specifying as it relates to principles involves making and defending predictions about what will or might happen under certain conditions. For example, a student is involved in the process of specifying by identifying what must happen or what might happen if the earth's orbit were a circle as opposed to an ellipse. The following question would elicit this type of thinking:

We know that the earth's orbit is elliptical and that there are certain things that happen on earth as a result. Assume, though, that the earth's orbit was a circle. What are some things that would necessarily change, and what are some things that might change? Explain the reasoning behind your predictions.

2. Specifying With Mental Procedures

Specifying, as it relates to mental skills and processes, involves identifying what must happen or might happen during the execution of the skill or process under specific conditions. For example, a student demonstrates knowledge specification by determining how the procedure of reading a bar graph would be altered if no legend was provided. The following question would elicit this type of thinking:

> How would you have to modify the process of reading a bar graph if no title was provided? Explain why your modifications are necessary.

The following question would elicit specifying relative to the mental process of writing:

> How would you have to modify the process of writing if you could not write multiple drafts? Explain why the modifications are necessary.

3. Specifying With Psychomotor Procedures

Specifying as it relates to psychomotor procedures is the same as specifying as it relates to mental procedures: Students identify what must happen or might happen in the execution of a procedure under certain conditions. The following task would elicit specifying relative to a psychomotor skill:

> Describe what would happen during a roundhouse kick in karate if the first movement you make when executing this kick is to raise the knee of your kicking leg as high as possible to your chest.

The following task would elicit specifying relative to a psychomotor process:

> Explain how you would have to modify your batting stance and batting technique to accommodate a pitcher who can throw a fastball 110 miles per hour.

LEVEL 4: KNOWLEDGE UTILIZATION

As the name implies, the knowledge utilization processes require that students apply or use knowledge in specific situations. In such cases, the student's mental activity is not focused on the knowledge per se, as is the case with the analysis processes. Rather, the student's mental activity is focused on a specific situation that is enhanced as a result of the knowledge. For example, while a student is engaged in the analytic process of analyzing errors relative to a principle about barometric pressure, the focus is on the information about barometric pressure. However, when using the knowledge of barometric pressure to help make a decision (a knowledge utilization process) about whether to stage a party indoors or outdoors, the focus is on the party as opposed to barometric pressure per se.

There are four knowledge application processes: (1) decision making, (2) problem solving, (3) experimenting, and (4) investigating. We consider each.

Decision Making

Decision making involves selecting among alternatives that initially appear equal. Figure 4.15 lists decision-making tasks across the three knowledge domains.

Figure 4.15   Decision-making Tasks

Information	
Details	When asked, the student uses his or her knowledge of details to make a specific decision or makes a decision regarding the details.
Organizing Ideas	When asked, the student uses his or her knowledge of a generalization or principle to make a specific decision or makes a decision regarding the generalization or principle.
Mental Procedures	
Skills	When asked, the student uses his or her skill at or knowledge of a mental skill to make a specific decision or makes a decision regarding the mental skill.
Processes	When asked, the student uses his or her skill at or knowledge of a mental process to make a specific decision or makes a decision regarding the mental process.
Psychomotor Procedures	
Skills	When asked, the student uses his or her skill at or knowledge of a psychomotor skill to make a specific decision or makes a decision regarding the psychomotor skill.
Processes	When asked, the student uses his or her skill at or knowledge of a psychomotor process to make a specific decision or makes a decision regarding the psychomotor process.

1. Decision Making With Information

Details are frequently employed as critical components in decisions. For example, students demonstrate the use of details to make decisions when they use their knowledge of specific locations to determine the best site for a waste disposal plant. The following question would elicit this type of thinking:

Assume that the following three sites are being considered as the location for a new waste disposal plant: (1) near the lake at the north end of town,

(2) near the airport, and (3) in the mountains outside town. Which site would be best? Explain why the specific characteristics of the site you selected make it the best selection.

Generalizations and principles are invariably key components of the decision-making process. Consider the foregoing example. It is true that details about the three locations are used to make the decision. However, it is also necessary to use generalizations or principles about waste disposal plants. Organizing ideas are generally the criteria one uses to make selections between alternatives. The following decision-making task would highlight the use of organizing ideas:

Your job is to determine who among the following individuals would be the best peacetime leader: (a) Martin Luther King, Jr., (b) Anwar Sadat, or (c) Franklin D. Roosevelt. Explain the criteria you used to select among the three.

To select among these alternatives, the student must use some form of organizing ideas—probably generalizations—about peacetime leaders, such as peacetime leaders should have a good understanding of similarities and differences between cultures.

2. Decision Making With Mental Procedures

Mental skills are sometimes used as explicit tools with which to gather information for decisions. For example, to elicit decision making that necessarily employs a specific mental skill, a student might be presented with a decision-making task such as the following:

Using the contour map of the region known as Four Corners, identify the best location to locate a water purification plant. Be sure to explain how the information in the contour map allowed you to select the best alternative.

Note that the directions to the task ask students to explain how the information in the contour map is useful in making the decision. Directions such as these are probably necessary to highlight the central role of a specific mental skill.

The following task would elicit the use of a specific mental process to make a decision:

Using the statistical program Ecostat as a tool, decide which of the three stocks we have been following in class would be the best long-term investment. Explain how the computer program aided in making this decision.

3. Decision Making With Psychomotor Procedures

Psychomotor skills and processes can be used when making decisions. However, the types of decisions in which they can be employed are somewhat restricted. Most commonly, the decision involves the best skill or process to use in a specific situation. For example, a decision-making task follows that involves specific karate skills:

> Which is the best kick to use against an opponent who has a strong front kick and side kick but a weak roundhouse kick?

The following decision-making task would make use of psychomotor processes:

> Identify which of the following processes is the best for you to rely on to win a point in tennis against a strong opponent:
> 1. Your ability to return a serve
> 2. Your ability to volley
> 3. Your ability to play the net

Problem Solving

The knowledge utilization process of problem solving involves accomplishing a goal for which obstacles or limiting conditions exist. Figure 4.16 lists problem-solving tasks across the three knowledge domains.

Figure 4.16   Problem-solving Tasks

Information	
Details	When asked, the student uses his or her knowledge of details to solve a specific problem or solves a problem regarding the details.
Organizing Ideas	When asked, the student uses his or her knowledge of a generalization or principle to solve a specific problem or solves a problem regarding the generalization or principle.
Mental Procedures	
Skills	When asked, the student uses his or her skill at or understanding of a mental skill to solve a specific problem or solves a problem regarding the mental skill.
Processes	When asked, the student uses his or her skill at or understanding of a mental process to solve a specific problem or solves a problem regarding the mental process.
Psychomotor Procedures	
Skills	When asked, the student uses his or her skill at or understanding of a psychomotor skill to solve a specific problem or solves a problem regarding the psychomotor skill.
Processes	When asked, the student uses his or her skill at or understanding of a psychomotor process to solve a specific problem or solves a problem regarding the psychomotor process.

Problem solving is closely related to decision making in that the latter is frequently a subcomponent of problem solving. However, whereas decision making does not involve obstacles to a goal, problem solving does.

1. Problem Solving With Information

Knowledge of details is commonly necessary to solve problems. For example, students might use their knowledge about a specific Broadway play to help solve a problem in its staging. To illustrate, consider the following task:

> You are putting on the play *Guys and Dolls* but have no money to build a set. In fact, you can use only boxes as the materials for your set. Draw a sketch of how you would stage a particular scene and explain how your use of the boxes is called for by that scene.

Within this task, it is a student's knowledge of a specific scene (i.e., a specific detail) within *Guys and Dolls* that provides the logic for stage design using boxes only.

Organizing ideas apply to a variety of problem-solving tasks. Commonly, a student uses a generalization or principle when identifying how best to overcome the obstacle within the problem. To illustrate, reconsider the problem about staging the play *Guys and Dolls*. It can be easily restated so as to emphasize a theatrical principle:

> You are putting on the play *Guys and Dolls* but have no money to build a set. In fact, you can use only boxes as your staging materials. Draw a sketch of how you would stage a particular scene. Explain how your use of the boxes is based on specific principles of set design.

The tool used to solve this problem is a specific principle or principles about set design as opposed to details about the musical.

2. Problem Solving With Mental Procedures

Specific mental skills can be vital to solving problems. For example, the following tasks require students to use the skills of mental computation and estimation:

> Your job is to build a fence that encompasses the largest span with 1,000 feet of two-by-four-inch planks. You must perform all computations and estimations mentally. You may not use a calculator or keep track of your calculations using paper and pencil. Explain how the use of estimation and mental computation affected your ability to solve this problem.

Note that the directions of the problem ask students to explain how the use of specific mental skills—in this case, estimation and mental computation—affect the problem-solving process.

Mental processes are tools that are frequently essential to solving a given problem. For example, the process of using a specific type of computer spreadsheet might be an integral aspect of overcoming a constraint in a given problem. Again, a task must be structured so as to make the process an integral part:

You have been supplied with a table that shows the following for a company you own: sales per week, unit price for production of new products, cash reserve in the bank, and overhead expenses broken down by various categories. Your job is to design a strategy to increase cash flow as much as possible in a six-month period. However, you cannot decrease or increase any of these variables by any more than 5 percent over the six-month period. You must use the spreadsheet program Excel that we have been studying. When you are done, explain how the use of Excel was involved in finding a solution to this problem.

3. Problem Solving With Psychomotor Procedures

Psychomotor skills and processes or knowledge of psychomotor skills and processes is used to solve problems that are fundamentally physical in nature. For example, a student might use his or her skill at serving to solve a problem in tennis:

You are going to play a match against someone who has exceptionally good ground strokes—backhand and forehand. You will be unable to use your forehand very much. What is your strategy?

The following task employs the use of psychomotor processes from the sport of basketball to solve a problem specific to that sport:

Your technique for guarding an opponent relies heavily on quick, lateral (side-to-side) movement on your part. However, you have pulled a muscle in such a way that it makes it difficult for you to move quickly to your right. What will you do to effectively guard an opponent who is your equal in terms of quickness but can't jump as high as you can?

Experimenting

Experimenting involves the generation and testing of hypotheses about a specific physical or psychological phenomenon. Figure 4.17 lists experimenting tasks across the three knowledge domains.

1. Experimenting With Information

Details are sometimes used as the basis for hypothesis generation and testing. For example, knowledge of details about the transportation system in

Figure 4.17   Experimenting Tasks

Information	
Details	When asked, the student uses his or her knowledge of details to generate and test hypotheses or generates and tests hypotheses regarding details.
Organizing Ideas	When asked, the student uses his or her knowledge of a generalization or principle to generate and test hypotheses or generates and tests hypotheses regarding a generalization or principle.
Mental Procedures	
Skills	When asked, the student uses his or her skill at or understanding of a mental skill to generate and test hypotheses or generates and tests hypotheses regarding a mental skill.
Processes	When asked, the student uses his or her skill at or understanding of a mental process to generate and test hypotheses or generates and tests hypotheses regarding a mental process.
Psychomotor Procedures	
Skills	When asked, the student uses his or her skill at or understanding of a psychomotor skill to generate and test hypotheses or generates and tests hypotheses regarding a psychomotor skill.
Processes	When asked, the student uses his or her skill at or understanding of a psychomotor process to generate and test hypotheses or generates and tests hypotheses regarding a psychomotor process.

a specific city might be used by a student to generate and test hypotheses about that system. The following question would elicit this type of thinking:

We have been studying the public transportation system for the city of Denver. Using these facts, generate and test a hypothesis about some aspect of that system.

Experimenting is particularly well suited to organizing ideas since these knowledge structures most readily lend themselves to hypothesis generation. For example, a psychology student might use an understanding of a principle about how people react to certain types of information to generate and test a hypothesis about the reactions of a group of peers to a specific type of advertisement. The following task would elicit this type of thinking:

We have been studying principles concerning how human beings react to certain types of information. Select one of these principles, then make a prediction about how your classmates would react to a specific type of advertisement. Be sure to explain the logic behind your predictions. Carry out an activity to test your prediction, and explain whether the results confirm or disconfirm your original hypothesis.

2. Experimenting With Mental Procedures

Mental skills and processes are tools sometimes necessary in the generation and testing of hypotheses. For example, use of the mental skill of reading the periodic table might be an integral part of an experimenting task:

> Using the periodic table, generate a hypothesis about the interaction of two or more elements. Then carry out an activity that tests the hypothesis. Report and explain your findings.

The following task would use the mental process of accessing the World Wide Web as a tool in experimenting:

> Using the World Wide Web as your source of information, generate and test a hypothesis about the types of Web sites that are developed by specific types of organizations.

3. Experimenting With Psychomotor Procedures

In certain situations, psychomotor skills and processes may be used as tools in experimenting. The following is an experimenting task that involves students' understanding of the psychomotor skill of hitting a wedge shot in golf:

> Generate and test a hypothesis about the use of a sand wedge in a situation where your golf ball rests on flat, hardened sand.

The following experimenting task involves the psychomotor process of playing defense in tennis:

> Generate and test a hypothesis about playing defense against a specific type of opponent in tennis.

Investigating

Investigating involves examining a past, present, or future situation. As explained in Chapter 3, it can be likened to experimenting in that it involves hypothesis generation and testing. However, the data used are not gathered by direct observation. Rather, the data are assertions and opinions that have been stated by others. In addition, the rules of evidence are different from those employed in experimental inquiry. Figure 4.18 lists the manner in which the knowledge utilization process of investigating applies across the knowledge domains.

Figure 4.18   Investigating Tasks

Information	
Details	When asked, the student uses his or her knowledge of specific details to investigate a past, present, or future event or conducts an investigation regarding the details.
Organizing Ideas	When asked, the student uses his or her knowledge of a generalization or principle to investigate a past, present, or future event or conducts an investigation regarding a generalization or principle.
Mental Procedures	
Skills	When asked, the student uses his or her skill at or knowledge of a mental skill as a tool to investigate a past, present, or future event or conducts an investigation regarding a mental skill.
Processes	When asked, the student uses his or her skill at or knowledge of a mental process as a tool to investigate a past, present, or future event or conducts an investigation regarding a mental process.
Psychomotor Procedures	
Skills	When asked, the student uses his or her skill at or knowledge of a psychomotor skill as a tool to investigate a past, present, or future event or conducts an investigation regarding a psychomotor skill.
Processes	When asked, the student uses his or her skill at or knowledge of a psychomotor process as a tool to investigate a past, present, or future event or conducts an investigation regarding a psychomotor process.

1. Investigating With Information

Knowledge of specific details is commonly the impetus for an investigation. For example, a student's understanding of details surrounding the assassination of John F. Kennedy might stimulate the student to find out what actually occurred. The following task would stimulate this form of investigation:

> We have been studying the 1963 assassination of John F. Kennedy. There are a number of conflicting accounts. Identify one of the conflicting accounts of this incident and investigate what is known about it.

Organizing ideas are very commonly the basis for investigations. For example, a student's understanding of a principle about the relationship between polar ice caps and ocean depth might be used as the basis for an investigation task such as the following:

> We have been studying the relationship between ocean depth and polar ice caps. Using your knowledge of these principles, investigate what might happen if the earth's temperature were to rise by five degrees over the next three decades.

2. Investigating With Mental Procedures

Mental skills are sometimes used as direct tools in investigations. For example, the skill of reading a specific type of map might be critical to a given investigation.

Study the provided contour map of Colorado in the year 1900. Use the information on the map as the basis for investigating why Denver became the largest city in the state.

Like mental skills, mental processes are sometimes used as tools in investigations. For example, the process of using a specific type of Internet database might be a tool necessary to an investigation task such as the following:

We have been using an Internet database that contains eyewitness stories from more than 5,000 survivors of the Holocaust. Using that database, investigate what you consider to be accurate and inaccurate accounts about what happened at Auschwitz during World War II.

3. Investigating With Psychomotor Procedures

Investigations might also be carried out about psychomotor skills and processes as shown by the following tasks:

Psychomotor skill: Investigate who first developed the jump shot in basketball.

Psychomotor process: Investigate who first developed the full-court zone press in basketball.

LEVEL 5: METACOGNITION

As described in previous chapters, there are four categories of metacognitive processes: (1) specifying goals, (2) process monitoring, (3) monitoring clarity, and (4) monitoring accuracy.

Specifying Goals

The metacognitive process of specifying goals involves setting specific goals relative to one's understanding of or skill at a specific type of knowledge and developing a plan for accomplishing the goals. Figure 4.19 lists tasks for specifying goals across the three knowledge domains.

As depicted in Figure 4.19, specifying goals not only involves setting goals for specific types of knowledge, but it also involves identifying how

Figure 4.19   Specifying Goals Tasks

Information	
Details	When asked, the student sets and plans for goals relative to his or her knowledge of specific details.
Organizing Ideas	When asked, the student sets and plans for goals relative to his or her knowledge of specific generalizations and principles.
Mental Procedures	
Skills	When asked, the student sets and plans for goals relative to his or her competence in a specific mental skill.
Processes	When asked, the student sets and plans for goals relative to his or her competence in a specific mental process.
Psychomotor Procedures	
Skills	When asked, the student sets and plans for goals relative to his or her competence in a specific psychomotor skill.
Processes	When asked, the student sets and plans for goals relative to his or her competence in a specific psychomotor process.

those goals might be accomplished. To demonstrate goal specification, a student must not only articulate a goal relative to a specific knowledge component but must also identify the specifics of a plan to accomplish the goal.

Questions that would elicit this type of metacognitive processing include the following:

Details: What is a goal you have or might have relative to your understanding of the 1999 conflict in Kosovo? What would you have to do to accomplish this goal?

Organizing ideas: What is a goal you have or might have relative to your understanding of Bernoulli's principle? How might you accomplish this goal?

Mental skills: What is a goal you have or might have relative to your ability to read a contour map? What would you have to do to accomplish this goal?

Mental processes: What is a goal you have or might have relative to your ability to use WordPerfect? How might you accomplish this goal?

Psychomotor skills: What is a goal you have or might have relative to your skill at making a backhand shot? What would you have to do to accomplish this goal?

Psychomotor processes: What is a goal you have or might have relative to your ability to play defense in basketball? How might you accomplish this goal?

It is the student's response to the question regarding the manner in which the goal will be accomplished that provides insight into the level at which a student is employing the metacognitive process of goal setting. For example, a response in which the student notes that "I will have to work harder" to accomplish this goal does not truly address the metacognitive process of goal setting. Rather, the student should identify a clear objective, a rough time line, necessary resources, and the like.

Process Monitoring

Process monitoring commonly involves determining how effectively a procedure is being carried out in real time, particularly when a goal has been established for the procedure. For example, a student is involved in process monitoring if, while playing defense in basketball, the student sets a goal for performance that day and then continually monitors which actions are effective, which are not, and what might be done to improve effectiveness. Process monitoring also applies to information. However, with this type of knowledge, the focus is on how well a learning goal is being accomplished relative to the information.

1. Process Monitoring With Information

As Figure 4.20 indicates, process monitoring for information involves monitoring the extent to which goals are being met in terms of understanding

Figure 4.20   Process-monitoring Tasks

Information	
Details	When asked, the student monitors how well a goal is being met relative to understanding specific details.
Organizing Ideas	When asked, the student monitors how well a goal is being met relative to understanding specific organizing ideas.
Mental Procedures	
Skills	When asked, the student monitors how well a goal is being met relative to the execution of a specific mental skill.
Processes	When asked, the student monitors how well a goal is being met relative to the execution of a specific mental process.
Psychomotor Procedures	
Skills	When asked, the student monitors how well a goal is being met relative to the execution of a specific psychomotor skill.
Processes	When asked, the student monitors how well a goal is being met relative to the execution of a specific psychomotor process.

specific details and organizing ideas. The following task examples elicit this type of thinking:

> Details: We have been studying the events of the attack on the World Trade Center in New York City in 2001. Pick some specific details regarding those events that you would like to understand better. As we progress, keep track of your understanding, and identify those things you are doing that enhance your understanding and those things you are not doing that might be helpful.

> Organizing ideas: We have been studying the principle of supply and demand. Select some aspects of this principle you would like to understand better. As we progress, keep track of your understanding, and identify those things you are doing that enhance your understanding and those things you are not doing that might be helpful.

2. Process Monitoring With Mental and Psychomotor Procedures

To elicit process monitoring for mental and psychomotor procedures, tasks must be designed in such a way that students can think about and monitor a skill or process while engaged in its execution. Commonly, situations must be contrived so that a student can execute the procedure but also have the opportunity to set a short-term goal relative to the execution of the procedure.

Tasks that would elicit this type of process monitoring include the following:

> Mental skills: Below are four problems that involve transforming fractions to ratios. First set a goal for your performance. As you solve these problems, describe how effective you are at performing this transformation, paying particular attention to those things you must change to be more effective at meeting your goal.

> Mental processes: Your task is to write a short letter, save the letter on your hard drive, then print it out using letterhead paper. All this is to be done using WordPerfect. First set a goal for your performance. As you perform the task, describe how effective you are at using WordPerfect, paying particular attention to those things you should change to be more effective.

> Psychomotor skills: Demonstrate the proper technique for stretching the hamstring muscles. First set a goal for your performance. As you perform the task, identify and describe how effectively you think you are executing this skill.

> Psychomotor process: In a moment you will be asked to play defense against another basketball opponent. Set a goal for your performance. Periodically we will stop the action and ask you to describe how effectively you think you are playing defense, paying particular attention to what you might do to improve.

Monitoring Clarity

As its name implies, monitoring clarity involves determining the extent to which an individual is clear about specific aspects of knowledge. Clarity is defined here as being free from indistinction or ambiguity. Stated in more positive terms, one who is clear about knowledge can recognize the distinctions important to that knowledge and ascribe precise meaning to each important distinction. For example, a student who has clarity about the concept of *central tendency* knows that the mean, median, and mode are different descriptions of central tendency and understands the meaning of each of these types. Figure 4.21 lists tasks for monitoring clarity across the three knowledge domains.

Figure 4.21   Monitoring Clarity Tasks

Information	
Details	When asked, the student identifies those aspects of details about which he or she has difficulty making distinctions or is uncertain.
Organizing Ideas	When asked, the student identifies those aspects of a generalization or principle about which he or she has difficulty making distinctions or is uncertain.
Mental Procedures	
Skills	When asked, the student identifies those aspects of a mental skill about which he or she has difficulty making distinctions or is uncertain.
Processes	When asked, the student identifies those aspects of a mental process about which he or she has difficulty making distinctions or is uncertain.
Psychomotor Procedures	
Skills	When asked, the student identifies those aspects of a psychomotor skill about which he or she has difficulty making distinctions or is uncertain.
Processes	When asked, the student identifies those aspects of a psychomotor process about which he or she has difficulty making distinctions or is uncertain.

As Figure 4.21 indicates, the metacognitive process of monitoring clarity applies to all three knowledge domains in approximately the same way. Questions such as the following can be used to stimulate this type of metacognitive thinking:

Details: Identify those things about the 1999 conflict in Kosovo about which you are confused. What do you think is causing your confusion?

Organizing ideas: Identify those aspects of Bernoulli's principle about which you are confused. Be specific about those areas of confusion. What don't you understand?

Mental skills: Identify those parts of the skill of reading a contour map about which you are confused. What do you think is causing your confusion?

Mental processes: Identify those aspects of the process of using the word-processing program WordPerfect about which you are confused. Be as specific as you can. What do you think is causing your confusion?

Psychomotor skills: Identify those parts of the technique for stretching the hamstring muscles about which you are confused. What do you think is causing your confusion?

Psychomotor processes: Identify those aspects of playing defense in basketball about which you are confused. What are the causes of your confusion? Be as specific as possible.

The more precise students can be about their areas of lack of clarity, the more they are exercising the metacognitive process of monitoring clarity. For example, one level of monitoring for clarity regarding the mental process of using WordPerfect would be demonstrated by a student response such as the following:

"I get confused when I try to center things."

However, a much deeper level of metacognitive awareness would be exhibited by the following response:

"I don't understand how you can go back and center a line in the middle of a document without losing all the margins that you have already set up."

Monitoring Accuracy

Monitoring accuracy involves determining the extent to which one is correct in terms of one's understanding of specific knowledge. Monitoring accuracy is distinct from, but related to, monitoring clarity. A student could be clear about some aspects of knowledge—have no ambiguity or lack of distinction—but, in fact, be inaccurate. Figure 4.22 lists tasks for monitoring accuracy across the three knowledge domains.

As Figure 4.22 illustrates, a critical aspect of monitoring accuracy is defending or verifying one's judgment of accuracy. This implies that students must not only make a judgment about their accuracy but must provide evidence for this judgment: They must reference some outside source as proof of their assessment of accuracy.

Figure 4.22   Monitoring Accuracy Tasks

Information	
Details	When asked, the student identifies and defends the extent to which he or she is correct about his or her knowledge of specific details.
Organizing Ideas	When asked, the student identifies and defends the extent to which he or she is correct about his or her understanding of a specific generalization or principle.
Mental Procedures	
Skills	When asked, the student identifies and defends the extent to which he or she is correct about his or her understanding of a mental skill.
Processes	When asked, the student identifies and defends the extent to which he or she is correct about his or her understanding of a mental process.
Psychomotor Procedures	
Skills	When asked, the student identifies and defends the extent to which he or she is correct about his or her understanding of a psychomotor skill.
Processes	When asked, the student identifies and defends the extent to which he or she is correct about his or her understanding of a psychomotor process.

Questions that elicit this type of metacognitive processing include the following:

Details: Identify those aspects about the 1999 conflict in Kosovo about which you are sure you are accurate and then explain how you know you are accurate. What is the evidence for your judgment of accuracy?

Organizing ideas: Identify those aspects of Bernoulli's principle about which you are sure you are correct. What is the evidence for your judgment of accuracy?

Mental skills: Identify those aspects of the skill of reading a contour map about which you are sure you are accurate. What evidence do you have for your judgment of accuracy?

Mental processes: Identify those aspects of using WordPerfect about which you are sure you are correct. What is the evidence for your judgment of accuracy?

Psychomotor skills: Identify those aspects of the process of stretching the hamstrings about which you are sure you are accurate. What is your evidence for your judgment of accuracy?

Psychomotor processes: Identify those aspects of playing defense in basketball about which you are sure you are correct. What evidence do you have for your judgment?

LEVEL 6: SELF-SYSTEM THINKING

As described in Chapter 3, self-system thinking involves four aspects: (1) examining importance, (2) examining efficacy, (3) examining emotional response, and (4) examining motivation.

Examining Importance

The self-system process of examining importance involves analyzing the extent to which one believes that specific knowledge is important. As explained in Chapter 3, if an individual does not perceive a specific piece of knowledge as important at a personal level, he or she will probably not be highly motivated to learn it.

Figure 4.23 lists tasks for the self-system process of examining importance across the three knowledge domains.

Figure 4.23   Examining Importance Tasks

Information	
Details	When asked, the student identifies the personal importance he or she places on details and analyzes the reasoning behind that judgment.
Organizing Ideas	When asked, the student identifies the personal importance he or she places on a generalization or principle and analyzes the reasoning behind that judgment.
Mental Procedures	
Skills	When asked, the student identifies the personal importance he or she places on a mental skill and analyzes the reasoning behind that judgment.
Processes	When asked, the student identifies the personal importance he or she places on a mental process and analyzes the reasoning behind that judgment.
Psychomotor Procedures	
Skills	When asked, the student identifies the personal importance he or she places on a psychomotor skill and analyzes the reasoning behind that judgment.
Processes	When asked, the student identifies the personal importance he or she places on a psychomotor process and analyzes the reasoning behind that judgment.

As depicted in Figure 4.23, the process of examining importance is fundamentally identical across the knowledge domains. This type of self-system thinking can be elicited by fairly direct questions such as the following:

Details: How important do you think it is for you to have knowledge of the events surrounding the assassination of John F. Kennedy in 1963? Why do you believe this, and how logical is your thinking?

Organizing ideas: How important do you believe it is for you to have an understanding of Bernoulli's principle? Why do you believe this, and how valid is your thinking?

Mental skills: How important do you believe it is for you to be able to read a contour map? Why do you believe this, and how logical is your thinking?

Mental processes: How important do you believe it is for you to be able to use WordPerfect? Why do you believe this, and how valid is your thinking?

Psychomotor skills: How important do you believe it is for you to be able to effectively stretch the hamstring muscles? Why do you believe this, and how logical is your thinking?

Psychomotor processes: How important do you believe it is for you to be able to effectively play defense in basketball? Why do you believe this, and how valid is your thinking?

It is the students' response to the two-part tag question illustrated in the foregoing questions that provides the greatest insight into their ability to engage in this type of self-system thinking. To effectively engage in the process of analyzing importance, students must not only be able to explain the reasoning behind why they believe something is important or unimportant, but they must also be able to examine the reasonableness or logic of these judgments.

Examining Efficacy

The self-system process of examining efficacy involves examining the extent to which individuals believe they can improve their understanding or competence relative to a specific type of knowledge. As explained in Chapter 3, if individuals do not believe they can change their competence relative to a specific piece of knowledge, they will probably not be motivated to learn it, even if they perceive it as important. Figure 4.24 lists tasks for examining efficacy across the three knowledge domains.

Again, it is not just the ability to identify the beliefs that underlie a student's perceptions, but it is also the student's ability to analyze the validity or logic of these beliefs that demonstrates this type of self-system thinking.

Figure 4.24   Examining Efficacy Tasks

Information	
Details	When asked, the student identifies the extent to which he or she believes his or her understanding of a specific detail can be improved and analyzes the reasoning behind these beliefs.
Organizing Ideas	When asked, the student identifies the extent to which he or she believes his or her understanding of a generalization or principle can be improved and analyzes the reasoning behind these beliefs.
Mental Procedures	
Skills	When asked, the student identifies the extent to which he or she believes his or her competence at a mental skill can be improved and analyzes the reasoning behind these beliefs.
Processes	When asked, the student identifies the extent to which he or she believes his or her competence at a mental process can be improved and analyzes the reasoning behind these beliefs.
Psychomotor Procedures	
Skills	When asked, the student identifies the extent to which he or she believes his or her competence at a psychomotor skill can be improved and analyzes the reasoning behind these beliefs.
Processes	When asked, the student identifies the extent to which he or she believes his or her competence at a psychomotor process can be improved and analyzes the reasoning behind these beliefs.

Questions that would stimulate this type of thinking relative to the three knowledge domains include the following:

Details: To what extent do you believe you can improve your understanding of the John F. Kennedy assassination? What is the reasoning underlying this belief, and how logical is your thinking?

Organizing ideas: To what extent do you believe you can improve your understanding of Bernoulli's principle? Why do you believe this? How reasonable is your thinking?

Mental skills: To what extent do you believe you can improve your ability to read a contour map? What is the reasoning behind this belief, and how logical is your thinking?

Mental processes: To what extent do you believe you can improve your ability to use WordPerfect? Why do you believe this? How reasonable is your thinking?

Psychomotor skills: To what extent do you think you can improve your skill at making a backhand shot? What is the reasoning behind this belief, and how logical is your thinking?

Psychomotor processes: To what extent do you think you can improve your skill at playing defense in basketball? Why do you believe this? How reasonable is your thinking?

Examining Emotional Response

The process of examining emotional response involves identifying what emotions, if any, are associated with specific knowledge and why those associations exist. As described in Chapter 3, negative affect can dampen a student's motivation to learn or improve at something, even if the student believes that it is important and has the requisite ability and resources.

Figure 4.25 lists tasks for examining emotional response across the three knowledge domains.

Figure 4.25   Emotional Response Tasks

Information	
Details	When asked, the student identifies any emotions associated with specific details and analyzes the reasoning behind these associations.
Organizing Ideas	When asked, the student identifies any emotions associated with a generalization or principle and analyzes the reasoning behind these associations.
Mental Procedures	
Skills	When asked, the student identifies any emotions associated with a mental skill and analyzes the reasoning behind these associations.
Processes	When asked, the student identifies any emotions associated with a mental process and analyzes the reasoning behind these associations.
Psychomotor Procedures	
Skills	When asked, the student identifies any emotions associated with a psychomotor skill and analyzes the reasoning behind these associations.
Processes	When asked, the student identifies any emotions associated with a psychomotor process and analyzes the reasoning behind these associations.

Questions that would elicit this type of self-system thinking in students include the following:

Details: What emotions, if any, do you have associated with the conflict in Kosovo? What is the thinking behind these associations? How logical is this thinking?

Organizing ideas: What emotions, if any, do you associate with Bernoulli's principle? What is your thinking behind these associations? How reasonable is your thinking?

Mental skills: What emotions, if any, do you associate with the skill of reading a contour map? What is your thinking behind these associations? How logical are these associations?

Mental processes: What emotions, if any, do you associate with the use of WordPerfect? What is your thinking behind these associations? How logical is your thinking?

Psychomotor skills: What emotions, if any, do you associate with the technique for making a backhand shot? What is your thinking behind these associations? How reasonable is your thinking?

Psychomotor processes: What emotions, if any, do you associate with playing defense in basketball? What is your thinking behind these associations? How logical is your thinking?

The key feature of this type of self-system thinking is the identification of a pattern of thinking or experiences underlying a given association along with the reasonableness of this pattern of thinking. There is no particular attempt to change these associations—only to understand them. This said, an argument can be made that awareness of one's emotional associations provides the opportunity for some control over them.

Examining Motivation

The final type of self-system thinking involves examining overall motivation to improve one's understanding of or competence in a specific type of knowledge. As described in Chapter 3, overall motivation is a composite of the other three aspects of self-system thinking—perceptions of importance, perceptions of efficacy, and emotional response. Examining motivation, then, can be considered an "omnibus" self-system process incorporating the other three aspects of the self-system. Figure 4.26 lists tasks for examining motivation across the three knowledge domains.

Questions that would elicit this type of self-system thinking include the following:

Details: How would you describe your level of motivation to increase your understanding of the conflict in Kosovo? What are your reasons for this level of motivation? How logical is your thinking?

Organizing ideas: How would you describe your level of motivation to increase your understanding of Bernoulli's principle? What are your reasons for this level of motivation? How valid are those reasons?

Mental skills: How would you describe your level of motivation to increase your ability to read a contour map? What are your reasons behind this level of motivation? How logical is your thinking?

Figure 4.26   Examining Motivation Tasks

Information	
Details	When asked, the student identifies his or her level of motivation to increase understanding of specific details and analyzes the reasoning for this level of motivation.
Organizing Ideas	When asked, the student identifies his or her level of motivation to increase understanding of a generalization or principle and analyzes the reasoning for this level of motivation.
Mental Procedures	
Skills	When asked, the student identifies his or her level of motivation to increase competence in a mental skill and analyzes the reasoning for this level of motivation.
Processes	When asked, the student identifies his or her level of motivation to increase competence in a mental process and analyzes the reasoning for this level of motivation.
Psychomotor Procedures	
Skills	When asked, the student identifies his or her level of motivation to increase competence in a psychomotor skill and analyzes the reasoning for this level of motivation.
Processes	When asked, the student identifies his or her level of motivation to increase competence in a psychomotor process and analyzes the reasoning for this level of motivation.

Mental processes: How would you describe your level of motivation to increase your skill at using WordPerfect? What are your reasons for this level of motivation? How valid are those reasons?

Psychomotor skills: How would you describe your level of motivation to increase your competence at making a backhand shot? What are your reasons behind this level of motivation? How logical is your thinking?

Psychomotor processes: How would you describe your level of motivation to increase your skill at playing defense in basketball? What are the reasons behind this level of motivation? How logical is your thinking?

Ideally, when students respond to questions like the foregoing, they consider all three self-system components that can affect motivation: They comment on the importance they ascribe to the knowledge, the level of efficacy they perceive, and any emotions they associate with the knowledge. They also explain which of these three factors dominates their motivation.

Summary

In this chapter, the six levels of the New Taxonomy were described in terms of their relationship to the three knowledge domains—information, mental procedures, and psychomotor procedures. Objectives were stated for each knowledge type at each level, along with questions and tasks that would elicit behavior with which each objective could be evaluated.

CHAPTER FIVE

The New Taxonomy as a Framework for Objectives, Assessments, and State Standards

This chapter and the next address specific uses of the New Taxonomy. Where the next chapter addresses the topics of curriculum design and thinking skills, this chapter addresses use of the New Taxonomy (1) as a framework for designing educational objectives, (2) as a framework for educational assessments, and (3) as a tool for enhancing state standards.

EDUCATIONAL OBJECTIVES

Certainly a primary use of the New Taxonomy is to provide a framework with which to design educational objectives. This was a fundamental motivation for the development of Bloom's Taxonomy. Indeed, a few years prior to the publication of Bloom's Taxonomy, Robert Travers (1950), in a book titled *How to Make Achievement Tests,* lamented that a taxonomy of mental processes was a prerequisite to the effective design of educational objectives:

> The basic difficulty in defining educational goals is due to the fact that psychologists have not yet developed a classification of human behavior which is useful for this purpose. A comprehensive taxonomy of human behavior which had a numerical value assigned to each category of behavior would simplify the educator's task. It would also provide teachers with a common language for discussing educational goals and ensure that those who used the same terms referred to the same concepts. (p. 10)

From the day it was released, Bloom's Taxonomy was the framework of choice for designing objectives. Airasian (1994) provided a detailed discussion of the theory and practice of educational objectives prior to and after Bloom's Taxonomy. He explained that it is no accident that Bloom's Taxonomy was dedicated to Ralph Tyler (1949a, 1949b), a researcher, assessment expert, and curriculum theorist whose ideas laid the groundwork for school reform efforts in the second half of the twentieth century. In fact, the dedication reads: "To Ralph Tyler, whose ideas on evaluation have been a constant source of stimulation to his colleagues in examining, and whose energy and patience have never failed us" (Bloom et al., 1956, p. iv). Airasian (1994) explains that Tyler's "research, writing, and collegial interactions afforded the basic intellectual structure from which [the Taxonomy's] authors proceeded. His work provided the justification for its development and helped to fashion the educational context which made it relevant" (p. 82). Tyler influenced the development of Bloom's Taxonomy in a variety of ways, perhaps the most noteworthy of which was to clarify the concept of an "objective" and link objectives to the design of effective achievement tests.

For Tyler, an objective should contain a clear reference to a specific type of knowledge as well as the behaviors that would signal understanding or skill relative to that knowledge. Prior to Tyler's recommendations, an objective was thought of as a general topic. For example, the topic of "probability," found within many current state standards documents, would have been considered an objective prior to changes initiated by Tyler. To develop assessments that measured competence in these general topics, test makers typically constructed items that "sampled" the information or skill within the general topic (i.e., objective). For example, relative to the general topic of probability, items might be constructed that addressed the probability of independent events, the probability of joint events, the relationship of probability to statistical hypothesis testing, and so on. Although these elements are related, they most certainly do not represent a homogeneous set. In general, the items that were designed for the sampling of content within a general topic were recall or recognition items focused on basic information. This practice was grounded on research in the early twentieth century (e.g., Tilton, 1926; Wood, 1923) that indicated that knowledge of the basic information regarding a general topic was a strong indicator of students' abilities to apply the knowledge within that topic. As Airasian notes (1994), "From these studies came the assumption that test items requiring recall of facts were valid surrogates for measuring more complex student behaviors such as reasoning with content or applying content in various ways" (p. 83). Tyler was instrumental in dispelling this notion. Airasian explains,

> Tyler reported on studies he conducted at Ohio State University that showed fairly low correlations between scores on memory tests and scores on tests of reasoning and application of principles. On the basis

of these studies he argued that there were many levels and distinct kinds of behaviors a student could be expected to manifest for any given content topic. These behaviors ranged from rote memory to considerably more complex mental operations. He further argued that if teachers desired their students to master non-rote behaviors, then it was necessary for them to measure these behaviors specifically and separately from the measurement of information, because one could not rely upon tests of information to provide a valid indication of a student's ability to apply, analyze, or interpret. (p. 83)

Tyler's insights and tight logic made it clear that educators must articulate objectives (as opposed to general topics) that specified the content and the behaviors associated with the content that were to be the focus of instruction. Three of Tyler's books spoke specifically to this issue (Tyler, 1949a, 1949b; Waples & Tyler, 1934).

In effect, Tyler's work created a mandate and provided the blueprint for a taxonomy like that developed by Bloom and his colleagues. Airasian (1994) and Anderson et al. (2001) are quick to note that Tyler's notion of an objective has specific qualities that differentiated it from other versions of the construct. Both cite the work of David Krathwohl (one of the coauthors of Bloom's Taxonomy) and David Payne (1971), which identified three levels or types of objectives: Global objectives are the most general. They are broad, complex areas and are typically referred to as *goals*. For example, "students will be able to apply basic properties of probability" would be considered a global objective or goal.

Instructional objectives are the most specific of the three types. In his book *Preparing Instructional Objectives,* Mager (1962) explained that a well-written instructional objective should include three elements:

1. Performance: An objective always says what a learner is expected to be able to do; the objective sometimes describes the product or result of the doing.

2. Conditions: An objective always describes the important conditions, if any, under which the performance is to occur.

3. Criterion: Whenever possible, an objective describes the criterion of acceptable performance by describing how well the learner must perform in order to be considered acceptable. (p. 21)

In the middle of the triad are educational objectives (Anderson et al., 2001). They articulate specific areas of knowledge but don't identify the performance conditions and criteria as do instructional objectives. However, they do articulate a mental operation to be performed on the knowledge.

The emphasis in Bloom's Taxonomy, the Anderson et al. taxonomy, and the New Taxonomy is on educational objectives. Anderson et al. explain, "Our framework is a tool to help educators clarify and communicate what they intend students to learn as a result of instruction. We call these intentions 'objectives'" (p. 23). In the New Taxonomy we adopt this same stance. Also, we adopt a similar convention to Anderson et al. in terms of how objectives are stated. Specifically, we use the following stem, *The student (or students) will be able to . . .*, plus a verb phrase and an object of the phrase. The verb phrase states the mental process (i.e., retrieval, comprehension, analysis, knowledge utilization, metacognition, self-system thinking) that is employed in the objective, and the object states the type of knowledge that is the focus of the mental process (i.e., information, mental procedure, psychomotor procedure). For example, the following qualifies as an educational objective: "The student will be able to identify similarities and differences in the processes of meiosis and mitosis." The objective focuses on informational knowledge—meiosis and mitosis—and use at Level 3 (Analysis: Matching) mental operation. Figure 5.1 provides general statements of objectives for each level of the New Taxonomy.

Using the general guidelines provided in Figure 5.1, designing educational objectives is a fairly straightforward process. The first step is to identify the type of knowledge that will be the focus of the objective. To illustrate, assume that a teacher is planning a unit of instruction on the general topic of central tendency in mathematics. The teacher would first determine what type of knowledge will be involved. Using his state or district standards as a guide, the teacher might determine that the unit will focus in part on the median. Relative to the topic of the median of a distribution of scores, the teacher might generate the following objectives.

Level 1: Retrieval

Recognizing: Students will be able to validate correct statements about the median.

Recalling: Students will be able to produce correct statements about the median.

Executing: Students will be able to compute the median for a set of scores.

Level 2: Comprehension

Integrating: Students will be able to describe the defining characteristics of the median.

Symbolizing: Students will be able to represent the important features of the median in some graphic or abstract fashion.

Figure 5.1   General Form of Educational Objectives for Each Level of the New Taxonomy

New Taxonomy Level	Operation	General Form of Objectives
Level 6: Self-system Thinking	Examining Importance	The student will be able to identify how important the information, mental procedure, or psychomotor procedure is to him or her and the reasoning underlying this perception.
	Examining Efficacy	The student will be able to identify beliefs about his or her ability to improve competence or understanding relative to the information, mental procedure, or psychomotor procedure and the reasoning underlying this perception.
	Examining Emotional Response	The student will be able to identify his or her emotional responses to the information, mental procedure, or psychomotor procedure and the reasons for these responses.
	Examining Motivation	The student will be able to identify his or her overall level of motivation to improve competence or understanding relative to the information, mental procedure, or psychomotor procedure and the reasons for this level of motivation.
Level 5: Metacognition	Specifying Goals	The student will be able to establish a goal relative to the information, mental procedure, or psychomotor procedure and a plan for accomplishing that goal.
	Process Monitoring	The student will be able to monitor progress toward the accomplishment of a specific goal relative to the information, mental procedure, or psychomotor procedure.
	Monitoring Clarity	The student will be able to determine the extent to which he or she has clarity about the information, mental procedure, or psychomotor procedure.
	Monitoring Accuracy	The student will be able to determine the extent to which he or she is accurate about the information, mental procedure, or psychomotor procedure.
Level 4: Knowledge Utilization	Decision Making	The student will be able to use the information, mental procedure, or psychomotor procedure to make decisions or make decisions about the information, mental procedure, or psychomotor procedure.
	Problem Solving	The student will be able to use the information, mental procedure, or psychomotor procedure to solve problems or solve problems about the information, mental procedure, or psychomotor procedure.
	Experimenting	The student will be able to use the information, mental procedure, or psychomotor procedure to generate and test hypotheses or generate and test hypotheses about the information, mental procedure, or psychomotor procedure.

(Continued)

Figure 5.1 (Continued)

New Taxonomy Level	Operation	General Form of Objectives
	Investigating	The student will be able to use the information, mental procedure, or psychomotor procedure to conduct investigations or conduct investigations about the information, mental procedure, or psychomotor procedure.
Level 3: Analysis	Matching	The student will be able to identify important similarities and differences relative to the information, mental procedure, or psychomotor procedure.
	Classifying	The student will be able to identify superordinate and subordinate categories relative to the information, mental procedure, or psychomotor procedure.
	Analyzing Errors	The student will be able to identify errors in the presentation or use of the information, mental procedure, or psychomotor procedure.
	Generalizing	The student will be able to construct new generalizations or principles based on the information, mental procedure, or psychomotor procedure.
	Specifying	The student will be able to identify logical consequences of the information, mental procedure, or psychomotor procedure.
Level 2: Comprehension	Integrating	The student will be able to identify the basic structure of the information, mental procedure, or psychomotor procedure and the critical as opposed to noncritical characteristics.
	Symbolizing	The student will be able to construct an accurate symbolic representation of the information, mental procedure, or psychomotor procedure differentiating critical and noncritical elements.
Level 1: Retrieval	Recognizing	The student will be able to validate correct statements about features of information (but not necessarily understand the structure of the knowledge or differentiate critical and noncritical components).
	Recalling	The student will be able to produce features of information (but not necessarily understand the structure of the knowledge or differentiate critical and noncritical components).
	Executing	The student will be able to perform a procedure without significant error (but not necessarily understand how and why the procedure works).

Level 3: Analysis

> Matching: Students will be able to identify the similarities and differences between the median, the mean, and the mode.

Level 4: Knowledge Utilization

> Problem Solving: Students will be able to solve problems that require an understanding and computation of the median.

These objectives address Levels 1.0 through Levels 4.0 of the New Taxonomy and are heavily weighted in terms of Levels 1.0 and 2.0. A very different unit would ensue if the objectives were at Levels 2.0 through 6.0. Of course, not including objectives at Level 1.0 would imply that the teacher assumes that all students can recognize, recall, and execute basic knowledge regarding the median.

THE NONPRESCRIPTIVE NATURE OF THE NEW TAXONOMY

The foregoing discussion brings up an interesting point about the New Taxonomy: It is not intended to prescribe the objectives that a school or district should adopt, only to articulate the range of possible objectives that a classroom teacher or an entire school or district might address. It is entirely possible that many or all of the elements inherent in the metacognitive and self-system processes might be considered beyond the purview or responsibility of education within a given classroom, school, or district. In fact, it is reasonable to assume that some teachers, schools, or districts might not wish to address objectives that deal with those systems. To illustrate, E. D. Hirsch (1996), popular advocate of what he refers to as the "core knowledge" curriculum, is highly critical of instructional objectives that deal with the metacognitive and self-systems. Hirsch gives four reasons why such objectives are problematic:

- [They] may interfere with the orderly development of adaptive problem-solving strategies.

- [They] may carry severe opportunity costs by usurping subject matter instruction.

- [They] may overload working memory and thus impair rather than help learning.

- All of these potential drawbacks may have the most adverse effects on slow or disadvantaged learners. (p. 139)

These objections notwithstanding, there are compelling reasons why metacognitive and self-system learning objectives might be included in a comprehensive listing of objectives for a given type of knowledge. First,

Hirsch (1996) fails to recognize the vast amount of research supporting the importance of metacognitive and self-system thinking to the learning process. In their analysis of some 22,000 studies on 30 instructional variables, Wang, Haertel, and Walberg (1993) found that instructional strategies that focus on metacognitive and self-system processes were second in terms of their effect on student achievement (strategies that focus on classroom management had the greatest effect on student achievement).

Further support is provided for the importance of the self-system and metacognitive system in a meta-analysis by Marzano (1998). The study involved over 2,500 effect sizes to ascertain which level of the New Taxonomy they addressed. For example, if an instructional strategy addressed student beliefs and attitudes, it was coded as employing the self-system. If an instructional technique addressed the establishment of instructional goals, it was coded as employing the metacognitive system. Last, if the instructional technique addressed the analysis of information, it was coded as employing the cognitive system. The findings of the meta-analysis are reported in Figure 5.2.

Figure 5.2   Meta-analysis of Instructional Strategies:
Effects of Three Systems of Thought on Knowledge Gain

System	ES	n	Percentile Gain
Self-system	.74	147	27
Metacognitive System	.72	556	26
Cognitive System	.55	1772	21

NOTE: ES = effect size; n = number of effect sizes.

As indicated in Figure 5.2, the average effect size for instructional strategies that use the cognitive system is .55, indicating that these instructional techniques produce a gain of 21 percentile points on the average in terms of students' understanding and use of knowledge. The average effect size for instructional techniques that employ the metacognitive system is .72, signaling an achievement gain of 26 percentile points. The average effect size for instructional techniques that employ the self-system is .74, indicating an achievement gain of 27 percentile points. This is the largest of the three. At least as indicated in this study, the self-system exerts more influence over learning than does the metacognitive system, which, in turn, exerts more influence over learning than does the cognitive system.

Second, these areas seem to be systematically excluded from educational practice despite their importance in the learning process. This is particularly true of self-system objectives. Garcia and her colleagues (Garcia & Pintrich,

1991, 1993; Pintrich & Garcia, 1992) note that the importance of the self-system in the learning process, although recognized by psychologists, has been virtually excluded from the instructional equation by educators.

Third, enhancing metacognitive and self-system thinking is central to developing self-regulation, which some psychologists assert should be a fundamental goal of education. As Bandura (1997) notes,

> A fundamental goal of education is to equip students with self-regulatory capabilities that enable them to educate themselves. Self-directedness not only contributes to success in formal instruction, but also promotes lifelong learning. (p. 174)

Last, there is growing evidence that the public at large is supportive of educational goals that address metacognitive and self-system thinking. To illustrate, in a study of public opinion as to which of 250 educational objectives were the most important for students to master prior to high school graduation, those rated in the top one-third contained a significant proportion of objectives that were related to self-system and metacognitive thinking. For example, the sixth-rated objective out of 250 was the ability to understand and maintain emotional health. (For a discussion, see Marzano, Kendall, & Cicchinelli, 1998; Marzano, Kendall, & Gaddy, 1999.)

Whether to include objectives that address metacognitive and self-system thinking is a decision that must be made by individual teachers, schools, or districts. Certainly not all content addressed during a unit of instruction is important enough to be addressed at all levels of the New Taxonomy. Indeed, Anderson et al. (2001) focus their attention on the cognitive aspects of learning: "Our focus on objectives does not encompass all possible and important learning outcomes, in part because we focus exclusively on cognitive outcomes" (p. 23).

On the other hand, if educators wish students to address a given knowledge component as comprehensively as possible or wish to develop self-regulatory skills in students, then metacognitive and self-system objectives should be overtly addressed.

A TOOL FOR DESIGNING ASSESSMENTS

Airasian (1994) explains that Bloom's Taxonomy was a useful tool for instruction, curriculum, and assessment. However, the late 1950s saw a heightened emphasis on the use of educational objectives as a tool for designing assessments. It is no surprise that the first large-scale use of Bloom's Taxonomy was as a template for assessment design. So, too, may the New Taxonomy be used to design assessments. When used for this purpose, it is useful to frame the levels of the taxonomy as shown in Figure 5.3, which lists generic questions and probes for each level.

Figure 5.3   Generic Questions and Probes for the Levels of the New Taxonomy

New Taxonomy Level	Operation	Generic Question or Probe for Assessment Design
Level 6: Self-system	Examining Importance	How important is this information, mental procedure, or psychomotor procedure to you? What is your reasoning? How logical is your reasoning?
	Examining Efficacy	How capable do you think you are to learn this information, mental procedure, or psychomotor procedure? What is your reasoning? How logical is your reasoning?
	Examining Emotional Response	What is your emotional response to this information, mental procedure, or psychomotor procedure? What is the reasoning behind your response? How logical is your reasoning?
	Examining Motivation	What is your overall level of motivation for learning this information, mental procedure, or psychomotor procedure? What is your reasoning? How logical is your reasoning?
Level 5: Metacognition	Specifying Goals	What is your goal in terms of learning this information, mental procedure, or psychomotor procedure? What is your plan for accomplishing the goal?
	Process Monitoring	What is working well and what is not working well relative to your plan for learning this information mental procedure, or psychomotor procedure?
	Monitoring Clarity	About what are you clear and about what are you not clear relative to this information, mental procedure, or psychomotor procedure?
	Monitoring Accuracy	About what are you accurate and about what are you inaccurate relative to this information, mental procedure, or psychomotor procedure?
Level 4: Knowledge Utilization	Decision Making	How can this information, mental procedure, or psychomotor procedure be used to help make a decision? What decision can be made about this information, mental procedure, or psychomotor procedure?
	Problem Solving	How can this information, mental procedure, or psychomotor procedure be used to solve a problem? What problem can be solved about this information, mental procedure, or psychomotor procedure?
	Experimenting	How can this information, mental procedure, or psychomotor procedure be used to generate and test hypotheses? What

New Taxonomy Level	Operation	Generic Question or Probe for Assessment Design
		hypotheses can be generated and tested about this information, mental procedure, or psychomotor procedure?
	Investigating	How can this information, mental procedure, or psychomotor procedure be used to investigate something? What can be investigated about this information, mental procedure, or psychomotor procedure?
Level 3: Analysis	Matching	How is this information, mental procedure, or psychomotor procedure similar to and different from other information, mental procedures, or psychomotor procedures?
	Classifying	To what general category does this information, mental procedure, or psychomotor procedure belong? What are subcategories of this information, mental procedure, or psychomotor procedure?
	Analyzing Errors	What errors, if any, have been made in the presentation or use of this information, mental procedure, or psychomotor procedure?
	Generalizing	What generalizations can be inferred from this information, mental procedure, or psychomotor procedure?
	Specifying	What predictions can be made and proven about this information, mental procedure, or psychomotor procedure?
Level 2: Comprehension	Integrating	What is the basic structure of this information, mental procedure, or psychomotor procedure? What are the critical versus noncritical elements?
	Symbolizing	How can the basic structure of this information, mental procedure, or psychomotor procedure be represented symbolically or graphically?
Level 1: Retrieval	Recognizing	Which of the following statements are accurate about this information, mental procedure, or psychomotor procedure?
	Recalling	What are some details about this information, mental procedure, or psychomotor procedure?
	Executing	Perform this mental procedure or psychomotor procedure.

If one is to design assessments, then assessment formats must be considered. Recent years have seen an expansion of the various types of data considered as valid assessments. To illustrate, each of the following types of data is currently being used for assessment in K–12 classrooms:

- Forced-choice items
- Pictographs, graphic organizers, charts, and graphs
- Essays and oral reports
- Performance tasks
- Teacher observations

It should be noted that the term *assessment* is being used in a specific way here. Indeed, before discussing the use of the New Taxonomy as a tool for assessment design, it is useful to define some common terms:

- Assessment: Gathering information about students' achievement or behavior
- Evaluation: The process of making judgments about the level of students' understanding or performance
- Measurement: Assigning marks based on an explicit set of rules
- Scores: The numbers or letters assigned to assessments via the process of measurement. The term *mark* is commonly used synonymously with the term *score.*
- Grades: The numbers or letters reported at the end of a set period of time as a summary statement of evaluations made of students.

As defined here, assessment is the collection of data that are used to make judgments (i.e., evaluations) about students, where judgment involves some kind of placement on a scale (i.e., measurement). With this in mind, it can be said that different types of assessment are most appropriate for different types of knowledge at different levels of the New Taxonomy.

In this section we address this issue for each of the five types of assessment listed. It is also important to note that our discussion addresses only the most direct use of these assessments. It is probably true that any type of assessment could be made to work with any type of knowledge at any level of the New Taxonomy; however, the following discussion addresses the optimum use of an assessment type for a given domain of knowledge and level.

Forced-choice Items

Measurement expert Rick Stiggins (1994) defines forced-choice items in the following way:

This is the classic objectively scored paper and pencil test. The respondent is asked a series of questions, each of which is accompanied by a range of alternative responses. The respondent's task is to select either the correct or best answer from among the options. The index of achievement is the number or proportion of questions answered correctly. (p. 84)

Stiggins (1994) lists four types of forced-choice items: (1) multiple-choice items, (2) true-false items, (3) matching exercises, and (4) short-answer, fill-in-the-blank items. As explained by Stiggins, short-answer, fill-in-the-blank items are counted in this category because they allow for only a single answer, which is counted either right or wrong. Teachers commonly use forced-choice items (along with essay items) to design their quizzes, homework assignments, midterm examinations, and final examinations. Such items play a major role in classroom assessment.

The utility of forced-choice items for the three knowledge domains across the six levels of the New Taxonomy is presented in Figure 5.4.

As depicted in Figure 5.4, forced-choice items are most appropriate for recognition of information for all three types of knowledge. To illustrate, consider the following sample items:

1. Information: A sodium ion differs from a sodium atom in that
   a. It is an isotope of sodium.
   b. It is more reactive than a sodium atom.
   c. It has a positive charge on its nucleus.
   d. It exists only in solution.
   e. It has fewer electrons.

2. Mental Procedures: Which of the following is the best description of the correct way to save a new file in WordPerfect?
   a. Use the mouse to click on the "File" command, then click on the "Save" command.
   b. The program automatically saves files when you exit.
   c. Type in the word *save* at the end of the file.
   d. After using the mouse to click on the "File" command, click on the "Save As" command.

3. Psychomotor Procedures: Which of the following is the best description of the correct way to hold a baseball to throw a curve ball?
   a. Keep index finger and middle finger wide apart and place them on the smooth part of the ball.
   b. Keep index finger and middle finger close together and place them over the seams of the ball.
   c. Keep index finger and middle finger close together and place them over the smooth part of the ball.
   d. Keep index finger and middle finger wide apart and place them over the seams of the ball.

Figure 5.4   Forced-choice Items

	Information	Mental Procedures	Psychomotor Procedures
Level 6: Self-system Thinking			
Examining Importance			
Examining Efficacy			
Examining Emotional Response			
Examining Motivation			
Level 5: Metacognition			
Specifying Goals			
Process Monitoring			
Monitoring Clarity			
Monitoring Accuracy			
Level 4: Knowledge Utilization			
Decision Making			
Problem Solving			
Experimenting			
Investigating			
Level 3: Analysis			
Matching			
Classifying			
Analyzing Errors			
Generalizing			
Specifying			
Level 2: Comprehension			
Integrating			
Symbolizing			
Level 1: Retrieval			
Recognizing	√	√	√
Recalling			
Executing			

Pictographs, Graphic Organizers, Charts, and Graphs

Pictographs, graphic organizers, charts, and graphs all emphasize symbolic representations of knowledge. The utility of these types of assessments for the three knowledge domains across the six levels of the New Taxonomy is depicted in Figure 5.5.

Figure 5.5   Pictographs, Graphic Organizers, Charts, and Graphs

	Information	Mental Procedures	Psychomotor Procedures
Level 6: Self-system Thinking			
Examining Importance			
Examining Efficacy			
Examining Emotional Response			
Examining Motivation			
Level 5: Metacognition			
Specifying Goals			
Process Monitoring			
Monitoring Clarity			
Monitoring Accuracy			
Level 4: Knowledge Utilization			
Decision Making			
Problem Solving			
Experimenting			
Investigating			
Level 3: Analysis			
Matching	√	√	√
Classifying	√	√	√
Analyzing Errors			
Generalizing			
Specifying			
Level 2: Comprehension			
Integrating			
Symbolizing	√	√	√
Level 1: Retrieval			
Recognizing			
Recalling			
Executing			

Given that pictographs, graphic representations, and the like all emphasize nonlinguistic over linguistic depictions of knowledge, they are, by definition, appropriate vehicles for determining the extent to which students can accurately symbolize knowledge. As noted in Figure 5.5, some forms of graphic representations are highly useful for assessing student competence in the analysis processes of matching and classifying, because both processes have specific types of graphic organizers devoted to them. To illustrate, Figures 5.6a and 5.6b contain examples of graphic organizers for matching and classifying.

Figure 5.6a   Matching Graphic Organizers

Characteristics	Items to be Compared			
	1	2	3	
1.				Similarities
				Differences
2.				Similarities
				Differences
3.				Similarities
				Differences
4.				Similarities
				Differences

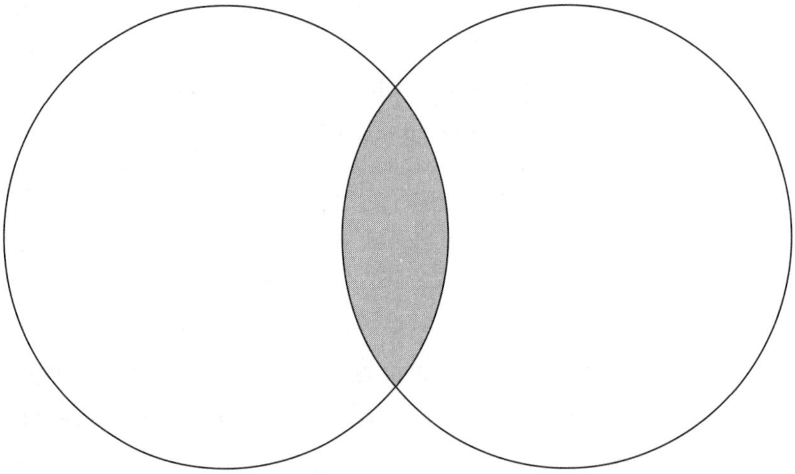

Figure 5.6b   Classifying Graphic Organizers

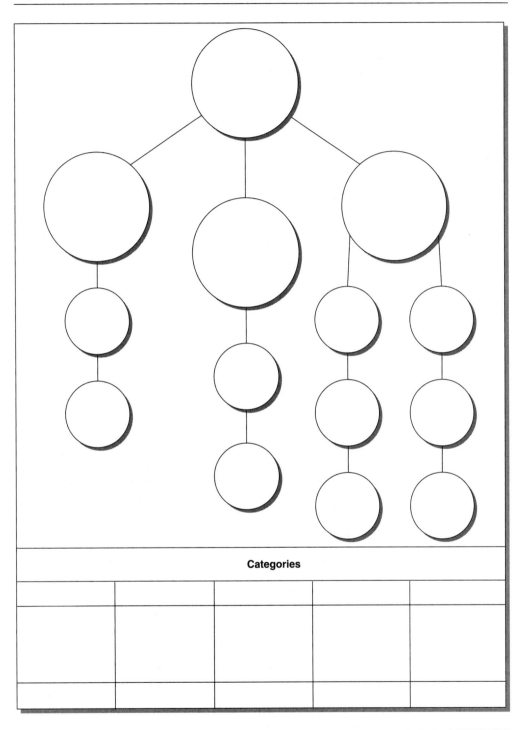

Essays and Oral Reports

Essays were probably the first form of assessment used in public education. Essays require students to construct their responses and therefore are highly useful for eliciting explanations. To help ensure that essays assess more than recall of information, the Center for Research on Evaluation, Standards, and Student Testing (CRESST) recommends that students be provided information that they can use and react to. To illustrate, CRESST provides students with the information in Figure 5.7 as part of a history essay question.

Figure 5.7   Background for Essay Items

	Excerpts From the Lincoln-Douglas Debate
Stephen A. Douglas	Mr. Lincoln tells you, in his speech made at Springfield, before the Convention which gave him his unanimous nomination, that "A house divided against itself cannot stand." "I believe this government cannot endure permanently, half slave and half free." "I do not expect the Union to be dissolved, I don't expect the house to fall; but I do expect it will cease to be divided." "It will become all one thing or all the other." That is the fundamental principle upon which he sets out in this campaign. Well, I do not suppose you will believe one word of it when you come to examine it carefully, and see its consequences. Although the Republic has existed from 1789 to this day, divided into Free States and Slave States, yet we are told that in the future it cannot endure unless they shall become all free or all slave. For that reason he says. . . .
Abraham Lincoln	Judge Douglas made two points upon my recent speech at Springfield. He says they are to be the issues of this campaign. The first one of these points he bases upon the language in a speech which I delivered at Springfield which I believe I can quote correctly from memory. I said there that "we are now far into the fifth year since a policy was instituted for the avowed object, and with the confident promise, of putting an end to slavery agitation; under the operation of that policy, that agitation had not only not ceased, but had constantly augmented." "I believe it will not cease until a crisis shall have been reached and passed. 'A house divided against itself cannot stand.' I believe this Government cannot endure permanently, half slave and half free." "I do not expect the Union to be dissolved"—I am quoting from my speech—"I do not expect the house to fall, but I do expect it will cease to be divided. It will become all one thing or the other. Either the opponents of slavery will arrest the spread of it and place it where the public mind shall rest, in the belief that it is in the course of ultimate extinction, or its advocates will push it forward until it shall become alike lawful in all the States, North as well as South. . . ."

With this information as a backdrop to which all students have access, the following essay item is presented:

Imagine that it is 1858 and you are an educated citizen living in Illinois. Because you are interested in politics and always keep yourself well-informed, you make a special trip to hear Abraham Lincoln and Stephen Douglas debating during their campaigns for the Senate seat representing Illinois. After the debates you return home, where your cousin asks you about some of the problems that are facing the nation at this time.

Write an essay in which you explain the most important ideas and issues your cousin should understand. (Baker, Aschbacher, Niemi, & Sato, 1992, p. 23)

Oral reports can be thought of as essays presented in oral form. The same characteristics that make for a good essay task make for a good task designed to elicit an oral report.

The extent to which essays and oral reports can be used to assess different types of knowledge across the six levels of the New Taxonomy is presented in Figure 5.8.

Essays can effectively provide assessment data for almost all types of knowledge across almost every level of the New Taxonomy, because essays and oral reports are ideal vehicles for the explanations and presentations of evidence that are required for every element marked in Figure 5.8. For example, explanations are required of students if they are to demonstrate competence in the self-system process of examining importance. Recall from the discussion in Chapter 4 that a question such as the following would elicit this type of thinking relative to the psychomotor process of playing defense in basketball:

How important do you believe it is to be able to play defense in basketball? Why do you believe this, and what is the reasoning behind your thinking?

To respond to this question, students would not only have to provide explanations but also would have to present coherent arguments for their explanations. Both aspects of the response could be communicated well via a written or oral report.

About the only aspects of the New Taxonomy for which essays and oral reports are not useful are the retrieval processes of recognizing, recalling, and executing and the comprehension process of symbolizing. By definition, these processes do not require explanations.

Performance Tasks

Performance tasks have become very popular as tools for assessment. One of their defining characteristics is that they require students to construct their

Figure 5.8   Essays and Oral Reports

	Information	Mental Procedures	Psychomotor Procedures
Level 6: Self-system Thinking			
Examining Importance	√	√	√
Examining Efficacy	√	√	√
Examining Emotional Response	√	√	√
Examining Motivation	√	√	√
Level 5: Metacognition			
Specifying Goals	√	√	√
Process Monitoring	√	√	√
Monitoring Clarity	√	√	√
Monitoring Accuracy	√	√	√
Level 4: Knowledge Utilization			
Decision Making	√	√	√
Problem Solving	√	√	√
Experimenting	√	√	√
Investigating	√	√	√
Level 3: Analysis			
Matching	√	√	√
Classifying	√	√	√
Analyzing Errors	√	√	√
Generalizing	√	√	√
Specifying	√	√	√
Level 2: Comprehension			
Integrating	√	√	√
Symbolizing			
Level 1: Retrieval			
Recognizing			
Recalling			
Executing			

responses and apply their knowledge (Meyer, 1992). To illustrate, consider the following performance tasks used by the National Assessment of Education Progress (for more examples, see Educational Testing Service, 1987).

1. Students are asked to describe what occurs when a drop of water is placed on each of seven different types of building materials. Next, they are asked to predict what will happen to a drop of water as it is placed on the surface of unknown material sealed in a plastic bag so that students can examine it but not test it.

2. Students are given a sample of three different materials and an open box. The samples differ in size, shape, and weight. The students are asked to determine whether the box would weigh the least (and the most) if it were filled completely with materials A, B, or C.

Researchers Fred Newmann, Walter Secado, and Gary Wehlage (1995) offer the examples in Figure 5.9 of performance tasks in geometry and social studies.

Figure 5.9   Performance Tasks

Geometry Task	Design packaging that will hold 576 cans of Campbell's Tomato Soup (net weight, 10 3/4 oz.) or packaging that will hold 144 boxes of Kellogg's Rice Krispies (net weight, 19 oz.). Use and list each individual package's real measurements; create scale drawings of front, top, and side perspectives; show the unfolded boxes and containers in a scale drawing; build a proportional, three-dimensional model.
Social Studies Task	Write a letter to a student living in South Central Los Angeles conveying your feeling about what happened in that area following the acquittal of police officers in the Rodney King case. Discuss the tension between our natural impulse to strike back at social injustice and the principles of nonviolence.

The extent to which performance tasks can be used to assess the three knowledge domains across the six levels of the New Taxonomy is depicted in Figure 5.10.

As shown in Figure 5.10, performance tasks are useful for all types of knowledge across all levels of the New Taxonomy except for recognizing and recalling. One reason for this is that performance tasks commonly incorporate essays and oral reports. Therefore, performance tasks can address any type of knowledge and any aspect of the Taxonomy that can be assessed using essays and oral reports. In addition, performance tasks can be used to demonstrate the execution of skills and processes where essays and oral reports cannot. For example, in a performance task, students might be able to demonstrate their ability to perform a specific psychomotor process, whereas this would be difficult in an essay or oral report.

Figure 5.10   Performance Tasks

	Information	Mental Procedures	Psychomotor Procedures
Level 6: Self-system Thinking			
Examining Importance	√	√	√
Examining Efficacy	√	√	√
Examining Emotional Response	√	√	√
Examining Motivation	√	√	√
Level 5: Metacognition			
Specifying Goals	√	√	√
Process Monitoring	√	√	√
Monitoring Clarity	√	√	√
Monitoring Accuracy	√	√	√
Level 4: Knowledge Utilization			
Decision Making	√	√	√
Problem Solving	√	√	√
Experimenting	√	√	√
Investigating	√	√	√
Level 3: Analysis			
Matching	√	√	√
Classifying	√	√	√
Analyzing Errors	√	√	√
Generalizing	√	√	√
Specifying	√	√	√
Level 2: Comprehension			
Integrating	√	√	√
Symbolizing	√	√	√
Level 1: Retrieval			
Recognizing			
Recalling			
Executing		√	√

Teacher Observation

One of the most straightforward ways to collect assessment data is through informal observation of students. Researcher Audrey Kleinsasser

(1991) explains that teacher observation involves the "informal conversations with students and observations of students that teachers make all day, every day" (p. 9). Reading expert Yetta Goodman (1978; Wilde, 1996) refers to this as "kid watching." Researcher Robert Calfee (1994; Calfee & Hiebert, 1991) attests to the validity of teacher observation if teachers are highly knowledgeable about the subject area they are observing.

Quite simply, teacher observation involves making note of students' understanding of and competence in specific knowledge components as students go about their daily business. This is probably the most unobtrusive way of collecting assessment data because teachers do not design and administer specific assignments or tests. Stiggins (1994) provides the following example of how a teacher might observe a student relative to social interaction skills:

A primary-grade teacher might watch a student interacting with classmates and draw inferences about that child's level of development in social interaction skills. If the levels of achievement are clearly defined in terms the observer can easily interpret, then the teacher, observing carefully, can derive information from watching that will aid in planning strategies to promote further social development. Thus, this is not an assessment where answers are counted right or wrong. Rather, like the essay test, we rely on teacher judgment to place the student's performance somewhere on a continuum of achievement levels ranging from very low to very high. (p. 160)

Figure 5.11 depicts the levels of the New Taxonomy for which teacher observation is most appropriate across the three knowledge domains.

Teacher observation is most appropriate for taxonomy processes that are easily observable over a short period of time. As Figure 5.11 illustrates, this limits its utility to retrieval (recalling and executing but probably not recognizing) and comprehension processes, since evidence of these can be quickly observed. For example, while walking about the classroom, a teacher might informally observe that a student accurately reads a bar graph or remembers a specific detail. However, it would not be easy to incidentally observe the conclusions drawn by a student as a result of classifying information or experimenting.

A STRUCTURE FOR ENHANCING
THE UTILITY OF STATE STANDARDS

What is often referred to as the standards movement in K–12 education can be viewed as an effort to identify what all students should know and be able

Figure 5.11   Teacher Observation

	Information	Mental Procedures	Psychomotor Procedures
Level 6: Self-system Thinking			
Examining Importance			
Examining Efficacy			
Examining Emotional Response			
Examining Motivation			
Level 5: Metacognition			
Specifying Goals			
Process Monitoring			
Monitoring Clarity			
Monitoring Accuracy			
Level 4: Knowledge Utilization			
Decision Making			
Problem Solving			
Experimenting			
Investigating			
Level 3: Analysis			
Matching			
Classifying			
Analyzing Errors			
Generalizing			
Specifying			
Level 2: Comprehension			
Integrating	√	√	√
Symbolizing	√	√	√
Level 1: Retrieval			
Recognizing			
Recalling	√	√	√
Executing		√	√

to do at various points in their schooling and to organize subject matter content into a spiral curriculum that supports their learning of this content. Although a complete discussion of the standards movement is beyond the scope of this text (for a detailed discussion see Marzano & Kendall, 1996a, 1996b), it is useful to briefly address its nature and function.

Many educators see the publication of the now famous report *A Nation at Risk* (National Commission on Excellence in Education, 1983) as the initiating event of the modern standards movement. Researcher Lorrie Shepard (1993) notes that, upon publication of the report, the rhetoric of education changed drastically. Proponents of reform began to make a close link between the financial security and economic competitiveness of the nation and our educational system. Who will soon forget the chilling words often quoted from *A Nation at Risk*: "The educational foundations of our society are presently being eroded by a rising tide of mediocrity that threatens our very future as a nation and a people. . . . We have, in effect, been committing an act of unthinking, unilateral educational disarmament" (National Commission on Excellence in Education, 1983, p. 5)?

These growing concerns about the educational preparation of the nation's youth prompted President George H. W. Bush and the nation's governors to call an education summit in Charlottesville, Virginia, in September 1989. Shepard (1993) explained that at this summit, President Bush and the nation's governors, including then-governor Bill Clinton, agreed on six broad goals for education to be reached by the year 2000. These goals and the rationale for them are published under the title *The National Education Goals Report: Building a Nation of Learners* (National Education Goals Panel, 1991). Two of those goals (3 and 4) relate specifically to academic achievement:

Goal 3: By the year 2000, American students will leave Grades 4, 8, and 12, having demonstrated competency in challenging subject matter, including English, mathematics, science, history, and geography; and every school in America will ensure that all students learn to use their minds well, so they may be prepared for responsible citizenship, further learning, and productive employment in our modern economy.

Goal 4: By the year 2000, U.S. students will be first in the world in science and mathematics achievement.

As one of the tools for accomplishing these goals, standards for what students should know and be able to do were drafted in all the major subject areas. Figure 5.12 contains a listing of the standards documents identified by national subject matter organizations.

In addition to the documents listed in Figure 5.12, 49 out of 50 states have identified state-level standards.

The common convention at the national and state levels is to define a standard as a general category of knowledge. Content standards primarily

Figure 5.12   National Standards Documents

Science	National Research Council. (1996). *National Science Education Standards.* Washington, DC: National Academy Press.
Foreign Language	National Standards in Foreign Language Education Project. (1999). *Standards for Foreign Language Learning in the 21st Century.* Lawrence, KS: Author.
English Language Arts	National Council of Teachers of English and the International Reading Association. (1996). *Standards for the English Language Arts.* Urbana, IL: National Council of Teachers of English.
History	National Center for History in the Schools. (1994). *National Standards for History for Grades K–4: Expanding Children's World in Time and Space.* Los Angeles: Author. National Center for History in the Schools. (1994). *National Standards for United States History: Exploring the American Experience.* Los Angeles: Author. National Center for History in the Schools. (1994). *National Standards for World History: Exploring Paths to the Present.* Los Angeles: Author. National Center for History in the Schools. (1996). *National Standards for History: Basic Edition.* Los Angeles: Author.
Arts	Consortium of National Arts Education Associations. (1994). *National Standards for Arts Education: What Every Young American Should Know and Be Able to Do in the Arts.* Reston, VA: Music Educators National Conference.
Health	Joint Committee on National Health Education Standards. (1995). *National Health Education Standards: Achieving Health Literacy.* Reston, VA: Association for the Advancement of Health Education.
Civics	Center for Civic Education. (1994). *National Standards for Civics and Government.* Calabasas, CA: Author.
Economics	National Council on Economic Education. (1996, August). *Content Statements for State Standards in Economics K–12* (unpublished manuscript). New York: Author.
Geography	Geography Education Standards Project. (1994). *Geography for Life: National Geography Standards.* Washington, DC: National Geographic Research and Exploration.
Physical Education	National Association for Sport and Physical Education. (2004). *Moving into the Future: National Standards for Physical Education* (2nd ed). Reston, VA: Author.
Mathematics	National Council of Teachers of Mathematics. (2000). *Principles and Standards for School Mathematics.* Reston, VA: Author.
Social Studies	National Council for the Social Studies. (1994). *Expectations of Excellence: Curriculum Standards for Social Studies.* Washington, DC: Author.

serve to organize academic subject domains through a manageable number of generally stated goals for student learning. For example, a synthesis of national- and significant state-level documents, McREL's online Compendium (Kendall & Marzano, 2005) identifies a number of standards that are common across science documents such as the following:

Science Standards

Earth and Space Sciences

1. Understands atmospheric processes and the water cycle
2. Understands earth's composition and structure
3. Understands the composition and structure of the universe and the earth's place in it

Life Sciences

4. Understands the principles of heredity and related concepts
5. Understands the structure and function of cells and organisms
6. Understands relationships among organisms and their physical environment
7. Understands biological evolution and the diversity of life

Physical Sciences

8. Understands the structure and properties of matter
9. Understands the sources and properties of energy
10. Understands forces and motion

Nature of Science

11. Understands the nature of scientific knowledge
12. Understands the nature of scientific inquiry
13. Understands the scientific enterprise

The content within each standard is then commonly further defined by more specific elements commonly called *benchmarks, indicators*, or *learning expectations*. Usually, multiple benchmarks are identified at grade level intervals. For example, Figure 5.13 contains benchmarks at four grade level intervals (K–2, 3–5, 6–8, 9–12) for the standard titled, "Understands atmospheric processes and the water cycle." When assigning benchmarks to grades, educators and content experts place academic content in a sequence for instruction that reflects what appears best for student learning. As the developers of *Benchmarks for Science Literacy* phrased it, benchmarks are organized with the intent to identify "the antecedent ideas . . . needed for students to make conceptual and psychological sense" of the concepts they are to learn (Project 2061, 1993, p. 304). The benchmarks in Figure 5.13, for example, suggest that students should understand the basic properties of water and the forms it takes before they are introduced to the water cycle.

The sequence in Figure 5.13 is akin to what Hilda Taba (1967) referred to as a "spiral curriculum." Its fundamental principle is that students are introduced to new knowledge in a rudimentary form at the earlier grades. At the higher grades the same knowledge is addressed in more depth and

Figure 5.13   Sample State Standards

Standard 1. Understands atmospheric processes and the water cycle

Level Pre–K (Grades Pre–K)

1. Knows vocabulary (e.g., rainy, windy, sunny) for different types of weather
2. Knows that weather conditions change over time
3. Knows how the environment changes over the seasons

Level I (Grades K–2)

1. Knows that short-term weather conditions (e.g., temperature, rain, snow) can change daily and weather patterns change over the seasons
2. Knows that water can be a liquid or a solid and can be made to change from one form to the other but the amount of water stays the same

Level II (Grades 3–5)

1. Knows that water exists in the air in different forms (e.g., in clouds and fog as tiny droplets; in rain, snow, and hail) and changes from one form to another through various processes (e.g., freezing, condensation, precipitation, evaporation)
2. Knows that the sun provides the light and heat necessary to maintain the temperature of the earth
3. Knows that air is a substance that surrounds us, takes up space, and moves around us as wind
4. Knows that most of earth's surface is covered by water; that most of that water is salt water in oceans; and that fresh water is found in rivers, lakes, underground sources, and glaciers

Level III (Grades 6–8)

1. Knows the composition and structure of the earth's atmosphere (e.g., temperature and pressure in different layers of the atmosphere, circulation of air masses)
2. Knows the processes involved in the water cycle (e.g., evaporation, condensation, precipitation, surface run-off, percolation) and their effects on climatic patterns
3. Knows that the sun is the principle energy source for phenomena on the earth's surface (e.g., winds, ocean currents, the water cycle, plant growth)
4. Knows factors that can impact the earth's climate (e.g., changes in the composition of the atmosphere; changes in ocean temperature; geological shifts such as meteor impacts, the advance or retreat of glaciers, or a series of volcanic eruptions)
5. Knows how the tilt of the earth's axis and the earth's revolution around the sun affect seasons and weather patterns (e.g., heat falls more intensely on one part or another of the earth's surface during its revolution around the sun)
6. Knows ways in which clouds affect weather and climate (e.g., precipitation, reflection of light from the sun, retention of heat energy emitted from the earth's surface)
7. Knows the properties that make water an essential component of the earth system (e.g., its ability to act as a solvent, its ability to remain a liquid at most earth temperatures)

Level IV (Grades 9–12)

1. Knows how winds and ocean currents are produced on the earth's surface (e.g., effects of unequal heating of the earth's land masses, oceans, and air by the sun; effects of gravitational forces acting on layers of different temperatures and densities in the oceans and air; effects of the rotation of the earth)
2. Understands heat and energy transfer in and out of the atmosphere and its involvement in weather and climate (e.g., radiation, conduction, convection–advection)
3. Knows the major external and internal sources of energy on earth (e.g., the sun is the major external source of energy; the decay of radioactive isotopes and gravitational energy from the earth's original formation are primary sources of internal energy)
4. Knows how the evolution of life on earth has changed the composition of the earth's atmosphere through time (e.g., the evolution of photosynthesizing organisms produced most of the oxygen in the modern atmosphere)

complexity. This notion has also been endorsed by Jerome Bruner (1960) and Patricia Murphy (1974). The examples in Figure 5.13 follow the general principles of a spiral curriculum. For example, in grades preschool through kindergarten, students are introduced to the notion that weather conditions can change. In grades K–2 this notion is revisited, this time adding the distinction of short-term weather conditions and seasonal weather patterns. In Grades 3–5 the distinction of forms of weather is introduced and so on.

Unfortunately, research indicates that many state standards documents do not adhere to this spiral format (see Kendall, Ryan, & Richardson, 2005). This is particularly the case when a standard involves mental procedures, such as "analyzing and using data." In such cases it is not uncommon for a standards document to simply restate the mental procedure at every grade level. The New Taxonomy can be useful in specifying different expectations for standards such as these. To illustrate, consider the standards developed in American Samoa (see Figure 5.14).

Figure 5.14   Using Taxonomic Levels to Support a Spiral Curriculum in American Samoa

	By the end of			
	Grade 1	*Grade 2*	*Grade 3*	*Grade 4*
Collects, organizes and reads data in charts, graphs and tables.	**The student** Knows ways to sort, represent, and compare objects using concrete materials (Level 1. Retrieval: Recalling)	**The student** Sorts data into categories and describes their relationships (Level 3. Analysis: Classifying)	**The student** Collects and organizes simple data using pictographs, tables, charts, and bar graphs. (Level 2. Comprehension: Representing)	**The student** Uses tables, charts, and graphs to make predictions and draw conclusions about data. (Level 3. Analysis: Specifying)

Source: Adapted from American Samoa (2004).

As evident in Figure 5.14, the mathematics standards in American Samoa indicate, in parentheses at the end of each statement, the level of the New Taxonomy that is appropriate for student learning. Thus the student should know a variety of ways to sort, represent, and compare objects at first grade, which is at Level 1: Retrieval. At second grade, the student should not only be able to sort but also describe how the categories used to sort relate to each other, which incorporates Level 3: Analysis. At third grade, students collect and organize data into charts and graphs (Level 2: Comprehension), and at fourth grade they use this skill to make predictions (Level 3: Analysis). Although the expectations at third grade are at a lower level in the taxonomy than second grade, the content is more challenging. This is because, as stated at the outset of this book, the difficulty at a particular level in the taxonomy is a function not only of the complexity of a given task but also the student's familiarity with the content or operation that is the focus of the task. In the case of third grade, the taxonomic level is lower than second grade, but the student is presented with a new skill for mastery—having to collect and represent data.

The New Taxonomy can be and has been used to revise benchmarks in a way that helps to shape the sequence of instruction, based on our understanding of how students learn. In this way, the New Taxonomy supplements other approaches to organizing benchmark content to support the development of a spiral curriculum.

In addition to being useful for revising benchmarks so that they help to support a spiral curriculum, the New Taxonomy can also be used to help clarify the intent of benchmarks. Across all three systems—the cognitive, metacognitive, and the self-system—the New Taxonomy maintains a distinction between the domain of information and the domain of procedures. Because this distinction affects every level of the New Taxonomy, no benchmark can be assigned a taxonomic level unless a choice has been made regarding whether the content of a benchmark contains information or procedures. This is an important question, though very often overlooked in the development of benchmarks. For example, consider the following benchmark:

> The student should be able to evaluate the credibility of an Internet health site.

This benchmark appears appropriate for Knowledge Utilization: Decision Making. However, the benchmark itself is ambiguous about what the student should learn. Examining the benchmark against the taxonomy helps to make the problem clearer (see Figure 5.15).

Depending upon whether the focus of the benchmark is determined to be information or procedure, we could expect two different kinds of teaching, learning and assessment. If the point of the benchmark is that students should know specific details or a set of basic principles about what to look for when deciding on the credibility of a health Web site, then the focus of teaching and learning would be on learning new information. However, if the intent of the benchmark is that the students should be able to evaluate a Web site for its credibility by applying a learned process, then the instructional emphasis would be on techniques and strategies applicable for evaluating a

Figure 5.15   Knowledge Utilization: Decision Making

Information	
Details	The student can use his or her knowledge of details to make a specific decision or makes decisions regarding the details.
Organizing Ideas	The student uses his or her knowledge of a generalization or principle to make a specific decision or makes decisions regarding the generalization or principle.
Mental Procedures	
Skills	The student can use his or her skill at or knowledge of a mental skill to make a specific decision or makes decisions regarding the mental skill.
Processes	The student can use his or her skill at or knowledge of a mental process to make a specific decision or makes decisions regarding the mental process.

site. Similarly, assessment would likely require the student to explain how the process used led to the decision regarding the credibility of the site. Once it is clear what the focus of the benchmark should be, it can be revised accordingly. First, the benchmark can be reworded. For example,

> The student knows what characteristics are common to credible Internet health sites

Or

> The student knows how to apply various criteria to determine the credibility of Internet health sites.

It is also possible to ensure clarity by adopting the approach illustrated in Figure 5.14, in which the benchmark is left unchanged, but the taxonomic level is indicated. For example,

> The student should be able to evaluate the credibility of an Internet health site [Decision Making: Information]

Or

> The student should be able to evaluate the credibility of an Internet health site [Decision Making: Mental Procedures].

Reviewing each benchmark in a state's standard document against the New Taxonomy can be used to make certain that the specific intent of the benchmark is clear and if it is not, to revise it in such a way that ambiguity is removed.

Summary

This chapter has addressed three related applications of the New Taxonomy. The first is as a framework for the design of educational objectives. A distinction was made between educational objectives versus instructional and global objectives. The second application is as a framework for designing assessments. Given that educational objectives have been specified, they should be assessed. The third application of the New Taxonomy is as a tool for enhancing and clarifying state standards.

CHAPTER SIX

The New Taxonomy as a Framework for Curriculum and Thinking Skills

As described in the previous chapter, the New Taxonomy has direct application to designing and assessing educational objectives as well as redesigning state standards documents. By direct extension, the New Taxonomy also is useful as a framework to guide curriculum design.

A FRAMEWORK FOR CURRICULUM DESIGN

When educators use the New Taxonomy to design objectives for a course, unit, or lesson, obviously they must then teach to those objectives. For example, assume that the following objectives were identified for a unit of study on World War II focusing on the use of atomic weapons by the United States.

Objective 1: Students will be able to recognize important people and events relative to the use of atomic weapons at Nagasaki and Hiroshima.

Objective 2: Students will be able to explain and symbolize the major events that led to the decision to use atomic weapons and the impact of that decision immediately after the use of the weapons.

Objective 3: Students will be able to examine the values and beliefs that led to the decision to use atomic weapons.

The first objective is at Level 1 (retrieval) because it requires students to recognize information about people and events important to the use of nuclear weapons at Nagasaki and Hiroshima. The second objective is at

Level 2 (comprehension) because it requires students to demonstrate an understanding of the overall pattern of events with an emphasis on comprehending the critical events that lead up to the use of nuclear weapons (integrating). Where the Level 1 objective requires knowledge of the pieces, the Level 2 objective requires knowledge of the whole. Given that the second objective requires students to explain and symbolize, it addresses both Level 2 operations: integrating and symbolizing. In effect, this objective is double-barreled. The third objective is at Level 4: knowledge utilization. It requires students to use the decision-making process to examine the events leading up to the use of nuclear weapons.

Once articulated, the objectives provide classroom educators with a sharp focus as to what must be taught. This clarity might also prove helpful in determining how it should be organized and sequenced. It is important to note that there is no single approach to the *how* component of this equation. One might say that there are three approaches to organization and sequencing instruction.

Approach 1: A Focus on Knowledge

In this approach the emphasis is on the introduction and acquisition of knowledge that is then expanded and extended. A unit organized under this approach would first address the Level 1 and Level 2 objectives—the retrieval and comprehension objectives, respectively. One might say that the tacit goal in this approach is new knowledge for its own sake. In the foregoing example, the intent under Approach 1 would be for students to recognize important people and events relative to the use of atomic weapons in Nagasaki and Hiroshima (Objective 1) as well as understand the major events in that episode of history (Objective 2). Typically, units organized this way progress from the specific to the general. Students are introduced to some factual knowledge about the use of nuclear weapons at Hiroshima and Nagasaki (Objective 1). Next the students are introduced to the bigger picture of the events leading up to, during, and after the use of nuclear weapons, providing an organizing framework for the episode (Objective 2).

Objectives that deal with Levels 3 and 4 of the New Taxonomy are instrumental objectives, in that their purpose is to deepen understanding of the Level 1 and Level 2 objectives. In this case students would be introduced to the concept that the use of nuclear weapons represented a decision that was made by a few key individuals and that decision provides evidence of the values and beliefs held by those who made the decision (Objective 3). To accomplish this objective, students might be presented with a task such as the following:

You are observing the interactions of those individuals who made the ultimate decision to drop the atomic bomb on Hiroshima and Nagasaki.

What are some of the other alternatives the committee probably considered? What criteria did they use to evaluate the alternatives, and what value did they place on those criteria that led them to their final decision?

The purpose of the task would be to deepen students' understanding of the events at Hiroshima and Nagasaki. In effect, the task would serve to add detail and sharpen understanding of this event.

Approach 2: A Focus on Issues

The same three objectives stated previously could be approached from the perspective of an emphasis on issues. Here the focus is on examining an issue or question that is relevant to past, present, or future issues. In this case, the third objective would be the centerpiece of instruction. To provide this focus, a Level 3 task would be presented to students at the outset of the unit. However, the task might be worded somewhat differently than the example for Approach 1:

Use of the atomic bomb on Hiroshima and Nagasaki during World War II was ultimately a decision made by a relatively small group of individuals. Part of your job throughout this unit will be to understand not only the people and events surrounding the use of nuclear weapons but also the values that guided those who made the decision. In addition, you will be asked to examine whether those values are still operative today. If you conclude that they are still present, explain how they affect current decisions made by those governing U.S. policy. If you conclude that they are not present, describe the difference between our current values and those present during World War II.

To accomplish this task, students must still accomplish Objectives 1 and 2, but the driving force of the unit is an issue or central question—what values led to the decision to use nuclear weapons and are they still present today? Wiggins and McTighe (1998) refer to such a question as an "essential question" and trace its use to John Dewey's (1916) view of schooling as the ultimate tool for a democratic society. In this approach the higher-level objective provides a reason for the lower level objectives: Objectives 1 and 2 are instrumental to accomplishing Objective 3. The lower-level objectives are not ends in themselves.

Approach 3: A Focus on Student Exploration

The third approach has student inquiry and self-analysis as its focus. Here the emphasis is on self-exploration as well as on knowledge of a subject area. In this case the unit of instruction might begin with a task such as the following:

> You are observing the interactions of those individuals who made the ultimate decision to drop the atomic bomb on Hiroshima and Nagasaki. What are some of the other alternatives the committee probably considered? What criteria did they use to evaluate the alternatives, and what value did they place on those criteria that led them to their final decision? After you have come to a conclusion as to the values that guided the decision, explain why you agree or disagree with those values. If you agree with those values, provide evidence for their validity. If you disagree with those values, identify the values you do agree with and provide evidence for their validity.

This task is obviously quite similar to the one provided under Approach 1 with the addition of the component that it asks students to identify whether they agree or disagree with the values exhibited by those who decided to use the atomic bomb. By definition, this third approach involves Level 6 (self-system) components. In this case students are being asked to examine importance—one of the four aspects of the New Taxonomy's delineation of the self-system. In effect, this approach explicitly or implicitly involves a fourth objective, which might be stated as follows:

> Objective 4: Students will be able to identify and analyze their beliefs and values as they relate to those underlying the decision to use atomic weapons at Nagasaki and Hiroshima.

The Three Approaches as Tools

While arguments have been made for the viability of one approach over another (see Caine & Caine, 1991; Carnine, 1992; Carnine & Kameenui, 1992; Hart, 1983; Hirsch, 1987, 1996; Kameenui, 1992; Lindsley, 1972; Wiggins & McTighe, 1998), our position is quite neutral. We view all three approaches as valid in different situations and with different students. Ultimately educators must select the approach that best meets the needs of the parents, guardians, and students whom they serve.

A Framework for a Thinking Skills Curriculum

One type of curriculum implied in the New Taxonomy is a "thinking skills" curriculum. As mentioned in Chapter 1, Resnick (1987) has outlined the rationale for teaching thinking. Since then, that rationale has be restated and elaborated by others (Costa, 2001; Costa & Kalick, 2000, 2004;

Halpern, 1996a, 1996b; Marzano, 1992; Marzano et al., 1988; Sternberg & Spear-Swerling, 1996). The need to teach thinking is also explicit in the state and national standards that have been developed (see Marzano et al., 1999).

Each level of the New Taxonomy identifies specific types of thinking that could be the subject of instruction. Students can be taught information and skills that enhance their ability to retrieve, comprehend, analyze, and so on. Before describing the specifics of such a curriculum, it is important to note that a common objection to the notion of teaching thinking is that human beings do not have to be taught to do something they do quite naturally. While this is obviously true, it is also true that human beings can be taught to perform an innate process more effectively. For example, all human beings can breathe without instruction, but it also true that human beings can be taught to breathe more efficiently and effectively. This is at the heart of a thinking skills curriculum—teaching students to engage in thought processes more efficiently, even though these processes might be innate abilities. Indeed, many researchers have demonstrated the tendencies to inefficient thinking (Abelson, 1995; Johnson-Laird, 1985; Perkins, Allen, & Hafner, 1983). On the lighter side of this issue, Gilovich (1991) identifies numerous illustrations of erroneous thinking in everyday reasoning, some examples drawn from those otherwise known to be rigorous academic thinkers. For example, Francis Bacon is reported to have believed that warts could be cured by rubbing them with pork. Aristotle thought that babies were conceived in a strong north wind. We might all be prone to peculiar errors, so even though the thought processes represented in the New Taxonomy are basic to human nature, people can benefit from overt instruction and practice in these processes.

Note that in the discussion to follow, we commonly recommend that students be provided with a set of steps or a protocol for various types of thinking. In cognitive psychology the term *protocol* typically refers to the use of subjects' explanations of what they are thinking at a given moment in time (see Ericsson & Simon, 1980, 1984). However, the term also refers to verbal descriptions of the steps or production rules that underlie a mental or physical procedure (Anderson, 1993). This later meaning is the one employed here: steps or heuristics that are presented to students to aid them in the initial stages of becoming more efficient at a given mental process. When used to this end, protocols are powerful scaffolds on which students develop and enhance their thinking effectiveness (Bodrova & Leong, 1996). Throughout this section we use the terms *steps*, *protocols*, and *strategies* somewhat interchangeably.

Level 1: Retrieval

As described in previous chapters, retrieval is the process of extracting information from permanent memory and depositing it in working memory.

Quite obviously, human beings engage in retrieval from birth. However, many techniques have been developed that enhance one's ability to retrieve knowledge. Most of those techniques posit the process of elaboration, which might roughly be described as linking new knowledge to old knowledge, mental pictures, physical sensations, and even emotions (see Hayes, 1981; Lindsay & Norman, 1977). A number of formal retrieval systems (sometimes referred to as mnemonic systems) have been developed, such as the rhyming pegword system (Miller, Galanter, & Pribram, 1960) and the method of places or loci (Ross & Lawrence, 1968). One of the most commonly used systems is the link strategy. Here, the learner creates a mental image for each piece of information he wishes to recall. He then links the images for each piece of information in a storylike format.

Level 2: Comprehension

Comprehension involves two related operations: integrating and symbolizing. Critical to integrating is recognizing the basic structure of information that is being processed. Researchers in the field of discourse analysis have identified many of the general patterns in which information is organized (see Cooper, 1983; Frederiksen, 1977; Meyer, 1975). As mentioned in Chapter 3 and shown again in Figure 6.1, some of the more common patterns found

Figure 6.1   Organizational Patterns

Characteristic Patterns	Organize facts or characteristics about specific persons, places, things, and events. The facts or characteristics need be in no particular order. For example, information in a film about the Empire State Building—its height, when it was built, how many rooms it has, and so on—might be organized as a simple characteristic pattern.
Sequence Patterns	Organize events in a specific chronological order. For example, a chapter in a book relating the events that occurred between John F. Kennedy's assassination on November 22, 1963, and his burial on November 25, 1963, might be organized as a sequence pattern.
Process-Cause Patterns	Organize information into a causal network leading to a specific outcome or into a sequence of steps leading to a specific product. For example, information about the events leading to the Civil War might be organized as a process-cause pattern.
Problem-Solution Patterns	Organize information into an identified problem and its possible solutions. For example, information about the various types of diction errors that might occur in an essay and the ways of correcting those errors might be organized as a problem-solution pattern.
Generalization Patterns	Organize information into a generalization with supporting examples. For example, a chapter in a textbook about U.S. presidents might be organized using this generalization: "U.S. presidents frequently come from influential families." It would be followed by examples of specific presidents.

in school-related materials are characteristic patterns, sequence patterns, process-cause patterns, problem-solution patterns, and generalization patterns.

These patterns can be taught to students and used as aids in the integration process; students can be taught the defining features of these patterns as tools in the process of integrating. With this background knowledge, students can be presented with the simple strategy of looking for explicit cues to the patterns. Once a pattern is discerned, it forms the basis for the organization and integration of the information. In effect, the protocol presented to students would be the following:

- Look for a pattern in the information.
- Once you have identified a useful pattern, organize the information using the pattern.

Strategies for the comprehension process of symbolizing might also be overtly taught (see Clarke, 1991; Heimlich & Pittleman, 1988; Jones et al., 1987; McTighe & Lyman, 1988). As depicted in Figure 3.3 in Chapter 3, each of the organizational patterns just described has a graphic organizer that can be used to symbolize it. Graphic organizers use language as well as symbols. Symbols are typically abstract in nature. To this end, pictographs can be presented as an alternative strategy to graphic organizers. A pictograph employs symbols and rudimentary drawings to represent information.

Level 3: Analysis

Analyzing involves five mental processes: matching, classifying, analyzing errors, generalizing, and specifying. The protocols for matching and classifying are similar in that they rely on the identification and analysis of characteristics. For both, students might first be presented with an explicit set of steps such as those shown in Figure 6.2.

Strategies like those depicted in Figure 6.2 have been suggested by Beyer (1988), Halpern (1996a, 1996b), Jones et al. (1985), Stahl (1985), and Taba (1967). It is worth noting that human beings match and classify quite naturally. However, it is also true that U.S. students have not done well on matching and classifying tasks. For example, in 1990 a National Assessment of Educational Progress report indicated that when U.S. students were asked to provide a written response contrasting the key powers of the president of the United States today with those of George Washington, only 40 percent of the 12th graders could muster at least two important characteristics, even though they were provided the basic information necessary to complete the task (Mullis, Owen, & Phillips, 1990, p. 24).

When applied to informational knowledge, analyzing errors involves identifying logical errors. Such errors have been described and catalogued by

Figure 6.2   Protocols for Matching and Classifying

Matching	Classifying
Select the items you want to match.	Select the item or items you want to classify.
Select the characteristics on which the items will be matched. Make sure the characteristics are important to the items and will help you better understand them.	Determine the defining characteristics of the item or items—those characteristics that make them what they are.
Describe how the items are similar regarding the characteristics.	Identify a category that the item or items belong to. Make sure that the item or items possess the defining characteristics of the category that has been selected.
Describe how the items are different regarding the characteristics.	If appropriate, identify subcategories of the item or items. Describe what makes the subcategories different from one another.
Summarize what you have concluded about the items.	Summarize what you have concluded about the item or items.

logicians and experts in the art and science of argumentation (see Johnson-Laird, 1983; Johnson-Laird & Bryne, 1991; Toulmin et al., 1981). Marzano, Paynter, and Doty (2003) have classified such errors into four broad categories, as depicted in Figure 6.3.

Given that students have a general understanding of logical errors, the following protocol for analyzing errors might be presented to them:

- Determine whether the information presented to you is intended to influence your thinking.
- If the information is intended to influence your thinking, identify things that seem wrong—statements that are unusual or go against what you believe to be true.
- Look for errors in the thinking that underlies the statements you have identified.
- If you find errors, ask for clarification.

When applied to procedural knowledge, analyzing errors involves identifying errors in a specific mental or psychomotor procedure. To illustrate, students are involved in analyzing errors regarding a mental procedure when they examine the process they use for solving algebraic equations because it frequently produces an incorrect solution. Likewise, students are involved in analyzing errors regarding a psychomotor procedure when they examine the process they are using to hit a baseball because it is not producing the results

Figure 6.3   Four Categories of Errors

---

1. *Faulty logic* can occur in seven different ways:

   - *Contradiction*—presenting conflicting information. If a politician runs on a platform supporting term limits, then votes against an amendment that would set term limits, that politician has committed the error of contradiction.

   - *Accident*—failing to recognize that an argument is based on an exception to a rule. For example, if a student concludes that the principal always goes to dinner at a fancy restaurant on Fridays because she sees him at one on a Friday that happens to be his birthday, that student has committed the error of accident.

   - *False cause*—confusing a temporal (time) order of events with causality or oversimplifying the reasons behind some event or occurrence. For example, if a person concludes that the war in Vietnam ended because of the antiwar protests, he is guilty of ascribing a false cause. The antiwar protests might have had something to do with the cessation of the war, but there were also many other interacting causes.

   - *Begging the question*—making a claim and then arguing for the claim by using statements that are simply the equivalent of the original claim. For example, if a person says that product x is the best detergent on the market and then backs up this statement by simply saying that it is superior to other detergents, he or she is begging the question.

   - *Evading the issue*—changing the topic to avoid addressing the issue. For example, a person is evading the issue if he or she begins talking about the evils of the news media when asked by a reporter about an alleged involvement in fraudulent banking procedures.

   - *Arguing from ignorance*—arguing that a claim is justified simply because its opposite has not been proven true. For example, if a person argues that there is no life on other planets because there has been no proof of such existence, he or she is arguing from ignorance.

   - *Composition-division*—asserting something about a whole that is really only true of its parts is *composition*; on the flip side, *division* is asserting about all of the parts something that is generally, but not always, true of the whole. For example, if a person asserts that Republicans are corrupt because one Republican is found to be corrupt, he or she is committing the error of composition. If a person states that a particular Democrat supports big government simply because Democrats are generally known for supporting government programs, he or she is committing the error of division.

2. *Attacks* can occur in three ways:

   - *Poisoning the well*—being so completely committed to a position that you explain away absolutely everything that is offered in opposition to your position. This type of attack represents a person's unwillingness to consider anything that may contradict his or her opinion. For example, if a political candidate has only negative things to say about an opponent, that is poisoning the well.

   - *Arguing against the person*—rejecting a claim using derogatory facts (real or alleged) about the person who is making the claim. If a person argues against another person's position on taxation by making reference to poor moral character, that is arguing against the person.

   - *Appealing to force*—using threats to establish the validity of a claim. If your landlord threatens to evict you because you disagree on an upcoming election issue, that is appealing to force.

3. *Weak reference* occurs in five ways:

   - *Sources that reflect biases*—consistently accepting information that supports what we already believe to be true or consistently rejecting information that goes against what we believe to be true. For example, a person is guilty of bias if he or she believes that a person has committed a crime and will not even consider DNA evidence indicating that the individual is innocent.

(Continued)

Figure 6.3 (Continued)

- *Sources that lack credibility*—using a source that is not reputable for a given topic. Determining credibility can be subjective, but there are some characteristics that most people agree damage credibility, such as when a source is known to be biased or has little knowledge of the topic. A person is guilty of using a source that lacks credibility when he or she backs up a belief that the government has a conspiracy to ruin the atmosphere by citing a tabloid journal known for sensational stories that are fabricated.

- *Appealing to authority*—invoking authority as the last word on an issue. If a person says, "Socialism is evil" and supports this claim by saying the governor said so, that is appealing to authority.

- *Appealing to the people*—attempting to justify a claim based on its popularity. For example, if a student appeals to his or her parents for a pierced belly button because everyone else has one, that is appealing to the people.

- *Appealing to emotion*—using a sob story as proof for a claim. For example, if someone uses the story of a tragic accident as a means to convince people to agree with his or her opinion on war, that is appealing to emotion.

4. **Misinformation** occurs in two different ways:

- *Confusing the facts*—using information that seems to be factual but that has been changed in such a way that it is no longer accurate. For example, a person is confusing the facts if he or she backs up a claim by describing an event but leaves out important facts or mixes up the temporal order of the events.

- *Misapplying a concept or generalization*—misunderstanding or wrongly applying a concept or generalization to support a claim. For example, if someone argues that a talk-show host should be arrested for libel after making a critical remark, the person has misapplied the concept of libel.

---

they desire. The general protocol for this type of analyzing errors might be stated as follows:

- Determine if the process you are using is working well for you.
- If not, carefully review the steps in your process. Consider the purpose of each step and whether you are performing that step well.
- Also consider other possible steps you might take.
- Try out different steps and different ways of performing specific steps until you obtain better results for the process.

Generalizing involves inferring unknown generalizations or principles from information or observations. Many of the discussions of this mental activity are presented in terms of induction (see Halpern, 1996a, 1996b; Mayer, 1992). As such, the protocols that typically are recommended are very robust in nature so as to include a variety of mental activities, some of which are addressed separately in the New Taxonomy (e.g., classifying and experimenting). As the description of generalizing indicates, we take a rather narrow perspective so as to provide a focus for instruction. A protocol that might be presented to students for generalizing, as defined in the New Taxonomy, involves the following elements:

- Focus on specific pieces of information or observations. Try not to make any assumptions about the information or observations.
- Look for connections between the information or for categories the information might fall into.
- Based on the connections you observe or the categories you've constructed, design a generalization.
- Reexamine your generalization to make sure that it fits with the information.
- Make corrections in your generalization as necessary and identify and state any exceptions to your generalization.

Specifying is the process of using information you know or assume to be true to infer unstated conclusions. The following is a protocol for specifying:

- Identify a general rule that applies to the current situation. Make sure the situation applies to all the conditions of the rule you have identified.
- What are some things that you know must be true or things you know must occur, given that the rule applies?
- Determine if the things you think must be true or must occur actually are true or occur.

Given that the protocols for the analysis skills will be new to most students, they must be taught. Beyer (1988) has proposed that thinking processes should be taught in a content-free environment: Instruction should focus on the protocols as opposed to the content to which the processes are applied. Conversely, Resnick (1987) and Glaser (1984, 1985) assert that protocols make sense only in the context of analyzing subject matter content. Although we agree with Beyer's emphasis on direct instruction, we hold the position that thinking protocols are best taught in the context of academic content. To this end, tasks such as the following would be presented to students:

The accumulation of waste materials is a growing problem in our society. Waste materials can be toxic, nontoxic, hard to get rid of, bulky, smelly, and so on. Imagine that you are on a task force formed by the federal government whose job is to classify various types of waste material. Using information we have learned in this unit, design a classification system. Make sure you include the following:

- Explain the logic behind each category in your system.
- Justify why each type of waste material belongs in the category to which you have assigned it.
- Explain why your system gets at the critical characteristics of waste materials.

This task requires students to address academic content as well as the process of matching.

Level 4: Knowledge Utilization

Knowledge utilization involves the application of knowledge in specific situations. In the New Taxonomy, knowledge utilization processes include decision making, problem solving, experimenting, and investigating.

Decision making is the process of selecting among alternatives that initially appear equal. A number of decision-making protocols have been developed (see Ehrenberg et al., 1979; Halpern, 1996a, 1996b; Marzano, Paynter, et al., 2003; Nardi & Wales, 1985; Wales & Stager, 1977). The following protocol incorporates many of the suggested elements:

- Identify the options or alternatives available to you.
- Identify the criteria a good decision will meet.
- Identify the alternative that best meets the defined criteria.

A more complex version of this protocol involves the weighting of criteria and the weighting of the extent to which each alternative meets each criterion. This allows for a quantitative estimate of the best alternative. The following is a protocol for this quantitative approach:

- Identify the options or alternatives available to you.
- Identify the criteria that will be used to make a good decision.
- For each criterion, assign an importance score (*absolutely necessary* = 3; *very important but not critical* = 2; *moderately important* = 1).
- For each alternative, assign a score indicating the extent to which it meets the criterion (*totally satisfies the criterion* = 3; *satisfies most of the attributes inherent in the criterion* = 2; *satisfies some but not most of the attributes inherent in the criterion* = 1; *doesn't satisfy any of the attributes inherent in the criterion* = 0).
- Multiply the importance score for each criterion by the score depicting the extent to which each alternative meets the criterion.
- For each alternative, add up the product scores. The alternative with the highest total score is the most logical choice.
- Based on your reaction to the selected alternative, determine if you wish to change importance scores for criteria or even add or delete attributes.
- If you have changed something, go back and recompute the scores.

Problem solving is the process of overcoming obstacles to accomplish a specific task. It is obviously related to decision making in that solving a problem typically involves making a decision, but the reverse is not necessarily true. Protocols for problem solving have been suggested by Marzano, Paynter, et al. (2003), Rowe (1985), Sternberg (1986b), and Wickelgren (1974). The following protocol contains many suggested elements:

- Identify your intended goal in concrete terms.
- List the obstacles in your way to accomplishing the intended goal.
- Generate a list of options for overcoming the obstacles.
- Determine which option is most likely to succeed, and try it out.
- If you first option doesn't succeed, try another option.

Marzano et al. (2003) have designed a more robust protocol that involves many of the metacognitive and self-system components of the New Taxonomy:

1. Determine whether you really have a problem. Is the goal truly important to you, or is it something you can ignore?

2. If you determine that you really do have a problem, take a moment to affirm the following beliefs:
   a. There are probably a number of ways to solve the problem, and I will surely find one of them.
   b. Help is probably available if I look for it.
   c. I am perfectly capable of solving this problem.

3. Start talking to yourself about the problem. Verbalize the thoughts you are having.

4. Start looking for obstacles in your way—what's missing? Identify possible solutions for replacing what is missing or overcoming the obstacles.

5. For each of the possible solutions you have identified, determine how likely it is to succeed. Consider the resources each solution requires and how accessible they are to you. Here is where you might have to look for help.

6. Try out the solution you believe has the greatest chance of success and fits your comfort level for risk.

7. If your solution doesn't work, clear your mind, go back to another solution you have identified, and try it out.

8. If no solution can be found that works, "revalue" what you are trying to accomplish. Look for a more basic goal that can be accomplished. (pp. 26–27)

Experimenting is the process of generating and testing hypotheses about a specific physical or psychological event. As mentioned in previous chapters, this knowledge utilization process is basically synonymous with what others refer to as scientific research, experimental research, and so on; however, it does not include the demanding rules of evidence and reporting associated with these more formal endeavors. Protocols have been suggested by Halpern (1996a, 1996b), Marzano (1992), Marzano et al. (1988), and Mayer (1992), among others. The following protocol contains many suggested elements:

- Observe something of interest to you and explain what has occurred. What rules, theories, or generalizations might explain what you have observed?
- Based on your explanation, what is a prediction you can make? What do you think would occur under which specific conditions?
- Design and carry out an experiment that will test out your predictions.
- Explain the results of your experiment in light of your explanation. Is there anything you have to change in your original explanation based on the findings from your experiment?

Investigating is the process of testing hypotheses about past, present, or future events. Marzano (1992) refers to these three types of investigating as *historical, definition*, and *projective investigation*, respectively. Historical investigation involves answering questions such as, What really happened? and Why did x happen? Projective investigation involves answering questions such as, What would happen if . . . ? and What would have happened if . . .? Definitional investigation involves answering questions such as, What are the important features of . . . ? and What are the defining characteristics of x? The following is a protocol that can be used with all three types of investigation:

- Clearly identify
    a. The concept to be defined (definitional investigation) or
    b. The past event to be explained (historical investigation) or
    c. The future or hypothetical event (projective investigation) to be defined or explained.

- Identify what is already known or agreed upon.
- Identify any confusions or contradictions.
- Develop a plausible resolution to the confusion or contradiction.

Just as with the analysis protocols, the knowledge utilization processes should be taught in the context of academic content. For example, experimenting might be taught and reinforced in the context of a task such as the following:

Identify something interesting you have noticed in an elevator. Explain what you have noticed using the principles we have studied in class about gravity, force, and motion. Based on your understanding of these principles, make a prediction that can be tested. Set up a study that will test your prediction. When you have completed your study, explain whether the results confirmed or disconfirmed your prediction. Make sure you report on specific information about gravity, force, and motion that we have addressed in class. Also include

- The rationale behind your hypothesis
- How your experiment actually tests your hypothesis
- How your results relate to your original hypothesis

Notice that the task asks students to report on the process of experimenting, along with the scientific principles that have been addressed.

Level 5: Metacognition

The metacognitive level of the New Taxonomy involves four types of thinking: specifying goals, process monitoring, monitoring clarity, and monitoring accuracy. Specifying goals involves establishing particular targets relative to one's understanding of information or goals relative to one's use of a procedure and a plan for accomplishing those goals. For example, a student is involved in specifying goals when deciding to understand the Bernoulli Principle by the end of the quarter and then establishing a plan for doing so. There are specific aspects to a well-set goal and a plan for accomplishing it that can be taught to students (Costa & Kallick, 2000, 2004). For example, students can be taught the following:

- Goals should include a concrete, identifiable behavior or event that will mark its completion.
- Goals should include an implicit or explicit plan for how it will be accomplished.
- The plan should identify the resources necessary to accomplish the goal.
- The plan should include milestones to mark progress.
- Frequently, goals must be altered or changed due to changing circumstances.

In addition, students can be made aware of situations when setting goals is particularly useful, such as the following:

- When they are taking on particularly challenging tasks
- When they are learning new skills
- When they are beginning new jobs
- When they don't feel adequately prepared for a task

Process monitoring involves keeping track of how well progress is being made toward the accomplishment of a goal. Many aspects of process monitoring have been identified as objects of direct instruction for students (Costa & Kallick, 2000, 2004; Zimmerman, Bonner, & Kovach, 1996). For example, students might be presented with general protocols such as the following:

- When involved in a difficult task, periodically stop and ask yourself these questions: How are things going? Could or should I be doing something differently?
- Periodically examine how close you are to attaining your goal.
- If you don't feel like you are making adequate progress on your goal, stop and examine your actions carefully and also assess how realistic your expectations of progress are.
- Periodically consider whether your goal must be changed.

The metacognitive processes of monitoring clarity and monitoring accuracy are often taught in tandem. They are obviously related in that effective thinking should be both clear and accurate (Barrell, 2003; Costa & Kallick, 2000, 2004; Halpern 1996a, 1996b). Relative to monitoring clarity, students might be taught information and strategies such as the following:

- Continually ask yourself, Am I clear about what is being presented to me? or Am I clear about what I am presenting?
- When you are unsure about what you want to say, rehearse it in your mind.
- When you are uncertain about the meaning of information, ask questions until you become more clear.

Relative to monitoring accuracy, students might be taught strategies such as the following:

- Before you state something as fact, make sure that you have the correct information.
- If you are not sure that something is accurate, qualify your statements indicating that to the best of your knowledge they are accurate.
- Develop the habit of stating how likely it is that statements are true rather than presenting them as simply true or false (e.g., "I'm very sure of what I just said but much more uncertain about what I am going to say next").

In addition to understanding and using these general protocols Halpern (1996a, 1996b) believes that students should be made aware of obstacles to clarity and accuracy that are frequently observed in human thought. These are depicted in Figure 6.4.

Figure 6.4   Common Errors That Influence Clarity and Accuracy

Awareness Regarding Obstacles to Clarity and Accuracy	Description
Regression toward the mean	Being aware that an extreme score on a measure is most commonly followed by a more moderate score that is closer to the mean
Errors of conjunction	Being aware that it is less likely that two or more independent events will occur simultaneously than it is that they will occur in isolation
Keeping aware of base rates	Using the general or typical pattern of occurrences in a category of events as the basis on which to predict what might happen in a specific situation
Understanding the limits of extrapolation	Realizing that using trends to make predictions (i.e., extrapolating) is a useful practice as long the prediction does not extend beyond the data for which trends have been observed
Adjusting estimates of risk to account for the cumulative nature of probabilistic events	Realizing that even though the probability of a risky event might be highly unlikely, the probability of the event occurring increases with time and the number of events

Level 6: Self-system Thinking

Providing instruction in the inner workings of the self-system is a topic that has received a considerable amount of attention over the past decade (Costa & Kallick, 2000; Goleman, 1995). As articulated in the New Taxonomy the self-system involves four related elements: examining importance, examining efficacy, examining emotional response, and examining motivation.

Examining importance involves analyzing how important a particular topic or event is to a student and why it is or is not perceived as important. To do so, a student must have an awareness of how importance is ascertained by human beings. Specifically, students might be made aware of the fact that at any point in time, a human being is trying to accomplish some implicit or explicit goal. As Glasser (1969, 1981) put it, we are goal-seeking mechanisms. Sometimes those goals have to do with basic human physical needs, such as being safe, well fed, and comfortable. Other times, those goals have to do with higher-level aspirations (Maslow, 1968; McCombs, 1984, 1986). Given that students have an awareness of these dynamics, a basic technique that can be taught to them is to identify the purpose of their behavior at any point in time, or stated differently, the goal their behavior will most likely lead to at any moment in time. This technique translates to asking and answering the questions, "What are the probable consequences of my actions right now, and is this what I want to occur?"

Examining efficacy involves analyzing and controlling the extent to which one believes he or she can accomplish a specific goal (McCombs, 1986; McCombs & Marzano, 1990; McCombs & Pope, 1994; McCombs & Whisler, 1997; Zimmerman et al., 1996). Seligman's (1990, 1994) work is particularly germane to the issue of teaching students to examine their sense of efficacy. Seligman notes that students should first be made aware of their explanatory style—how they explain success versus failure. In very broad terms, of the various ways to explain success, effort (or the "effort attribution") is the most powerful. If students cultivate the belief that effort breeds success, by definition, they will increase their sense of efficacy regarding challenging tasks.

Examining emotional response initially involves an awareness of the impact emotions have on human thought and human behavior (Goleman, 1995; LeDoux, 1996). Although the nature and function of emotions is a complex topic, for instructional purposes students can be presented with the simple model that there are four basic emotions: glad, sad, mad, and afraid (Marzano, Gaddy, Foseid, Foseid, & Marzano, 2005). Each of these emotions affects how we think and how we act. With this awareness students can be presented with techniques for monitoring the effects of their emotions on their thoughts and behavior and dampening the negative impact of some emotions, particularly strong emotions. To this end the following questions provide students with an awareness and potential control over their emotional responses:

- When you feel that you are particularly upset, try to notice what you are thinking and the conclusions you are coming to. Are they the same thoughts and conclusions you would come to if you weren't upset?
- When you notice that you are upset and not thinking clearly, take a time out from what you are doing. Go back to the situation when you have calmed down.
- When you are upset and interacting with someone, be very careful about what you say. You might regret comments you make because of your emotional state.
- If you find that you are upset regularly, try to figure out what is causing your emotions.

Examining motivation involves an awareness of one's overall level of motivation for a specific task. As the foregoing discussion and those in Chapters 1 and 2 indicate, motivation in a given situation might be thought of as the aggregate influence of the importance one ascribes to a given task, one's sense of efficacy regarding the task, and one's emotional response at that moment in time. Certainly, examining importance, efficacy, and emotional response in themselves go a long way to enhancing motivation. However, as a coordinated dynamic, motivation is under a student's control when it is recognized as a decision as opposed to a reaction on their part. Students can be presented with the notion that being aware of their thoughts regarding the importance of a task, their sense of efficacy about it, and their emotional response to it provides them with some control over their level of motivation in a given situation. With this awareness in place, students can be presented with the simple strategy of asking and answering the following question as a technique for monitoring their overall motivation: "Is my level of motivation sufficient to obtain the results I desire in this situation?" If the answer to this question is negative, the student can make the necessary alterations in one or more of the constituent elements: ascribed importance, sense of efficacy, and emotional response.

SUMMARY

This chapter first addressed the applications of the New Taxonomy to curriculum design. This is a natural consequence of the New Taxonomy's use as a tool for designing educational objectives. Once objectives have been created, the question arises as to how the curriculum will be designed to allow students to meet these objectives. Three models were presented, each with different emphases: a focus on knowledge, a focus on issues, and a focus on student exploration. Another way in which the New Taxonomy might influence curriculum is as a framework for teaching thinking. Each level of the New Taxonomy and each process within each level represents a legitimate and viable instruction.

Epilogue

This volume has presented the New Taxonomy of Educational Objectives. Educators are encouraged to use the New Taxonomy in ways they see fit, whether or not these ways are explicitly addressed in this book. In addition, the New Taxonomy is offered as a guide to educational reform, particularly in terms of the discussions regarding metacognitive and self-system thinking. Not only can objectives be designed for these processes but related knowledge and skills can be explicitly taught. While the New Taxonomy might be legitimately used without attention to these areas, it is our belief that they hold the potential of extending the influence of K–12 education into skill areas that are necessary for success in the twenty-first century.

References

Abelson, R. P. (1995). *Statistics as principled argument.* Mahwah, NJ: Lawrence Erlbaum.

Aiken, F. (1991). *The nature of science.* Portsmouth, NH: Heinemann.

Ainsworth, L. (2003a). *Power standards: Identifying the standards that matter most.* Denver, CO: Advance Learning Press.

Ainsworth, L. (2003b). *Unwrapping the standards: A simple process to make standards manageable.* Denver, CO: Advance Learning Press.

Airasian, P. W. (1987). State mandated testing and educational reform: Context and consequences. *American Journal of Education, 95*(3), 392–412.

Airasian, P. W. (1994). The impact of the taxonomy on testing and evaluation. In L. W. Anderson & L. A. Sosniak (Eds.), *Bloom's taxonomy: A forty-year retrospective: Ninety-third yearbook of the National Society for the Study of Education* (pp. 82–102). Chicago: University of Chicago Press.

Ajzen, I. (1985). From intentions to actions: A theory of planned behavior. In J. Kuhl & J. Beckman (Eds.), *Action-control: From cognition to behavior.* Heidelberg, Germany: Springer.

Ajzen, I., & Fishbein, M. (1977). Attitude-behavior relations: A theoretical analysis and review of empirical research. *Psychological Bulletin, 84,* 888–918.

Ajzen, I., & Fishbein, M. (1980). *Understanding attitudes and predicting social behavior.* Englewood Cliffs, NJ: Prentice Hall.

Ajzen, I., & Madden, T. J. (1986). Prediction of goal-directed behavior: Attitudes, intentions, and perceived behavioral control. *Journal of Experimental Social Psychology, 22,* 453–474.

Amabile, T. M. (1983). *The social psychology of creativity.* New York: Springer.

American Samoa Department of Education. (April 2004). *Mathematics content standards for grades 1-12.* Pago Pago, American Samoa: Author.

Anderson, J. R. (1983). *The architecture of cognition.* Cambridge, MA: Harvard University Press.

Anderson, J. R. (1990a). *The adaptive character of thought.* Hillsdale, NJ: Lawrence Erlbaum.

Anderson, J. R. (1990b). *Cognitive psychology and its implications* (3rd ed.). New York: Freeman.

Anderson, J. R. (1993). *Rules of the mind.* Mahwah, NJ: Lawrence Erlbaum.

Anderson, J. R. (1995). *Learning and memory: An integrated approach.* New York: John Wiley.

Anderson, L.W., Krathwohl, D. R., Airasian, P. W., Cruikshank, K. A., Mayer, R. E., Pintrich, P. R., et al. (Eds.). (2001). *A taxonomy for learning, teaching, and assessing: A revision of Bloom's taxonomy of educational objectives.* New York: Longman.

Anderson, L. W., & Sosniak, L. A. (Eds.). (1994). *Bloom's taxonomy: A forty-year retrospective: Ninety-third yearbook of the National Society for the Study of Education.* Chicago: University of Chicago Press.

Baker, E. L., Aschbacher, P. R., Niemi, D., & Sato, E. (1992). *CRESST performance assessment models: Assessing content area explanations.* Los Angeles: University of California, National Center for Research on Evaluation, Standards, and Student Testing.

Bandura, A. (1977). Self-efficacy: Toward a unifying theory of behavioral change. *Psychological Review, 84*(2), 191–215.

Bandura, A. (1982). Self-efficacy mechanism in human agency. *American Psychologist, 37,* 122–147.

Bandura, A. (1991). Social cognitive theory of self-regulation. *Organizational Behavior and Human Decision Processes, 50,* 248–287.

Bandura, A. (1993). Perceived self-efficacy in cognitive development and functioning. *Educational Psychologist, 28,* 117–148.

Bandura, A. (1996). Ontological and epistemological terrains revisited. *Journal of Behavior Therapy and Experimental Psychiatry, 27,* 323–345.

Bandura, A. (1997). *Self-efficacy: The exercise of control.* New York: Freeman.

Baron, J. (1982). Personality and intelligence. In R. J. Sternberg (Ed.), *Handbook of human intelligence* (pp. 308–351). London: Cambridge University Press.

Baron, J. (1985). Assessing higher order thinking skills in Connecticut. In C. P. Kearney (Ed.), *Assessing higher order thinking skills* (ERIC/TIME Resort 90). Princeton, NJ: Educational Testing Service.

Baron, J., & Brown, R. V. (Eds.). (1991). *Teaching decision making to adolescents.* Mahwah, NJ: Lawrence Erlbaum.

Barrell, J. (2003). *Developing more curious minds.* Alexandria, VA: Association for Supervision and Curriculum Development.

Beyer, B. K. (1988). *Developing a thinking skills program.* Boston: Allyn & Bacon.

Bloom, B. S. (1976). *Human characteristics and school learning.* New York: McGraw-Hill.

Bloom, B. S., Engelhart, M. D., Furst, E. J., Hill, W. H., & Krathwohl, D. R. (Eds.). (1956). *Taxonomy of educational objectivities: The classification of educational goals. Handbook I: Cognitive domain.* New York: David McKay.

Bodrova, E., & Leong, D. J. (1996). *Tools of mind: The Vygotskian approach to early childhood education.* Englewood Cliffs, NJ: Prentice Hall

Braine, M. D. S. (1978). On the relation between the natural logic of reasoning and standard logic. *Psychological Review, 85,* 1–21.

Brandt, R. (Ed.). (1986, May). Frameworks for teaching thinking [Special issue]. *Educational Leadership, 43*(8).

Brown, A. L. (1978). Knowing when, where and how to remember: A problem of metacognition. In R. Glaser (Ed.), *Advances in instructional psychology* (Vol. 1, pp. 77–165). Hillsdale, NJ: Lawrence Erlbaum.

Brown, A. L. (1980). Metacognitive development and reading. In R. J. Spiro, B. C. Bruce, & W. F. Brewer (Eds.), *Theoretical issues in reading comprehension* (pp. 453–481). Hillsdale, NJ: Lawrence Erlbaum.

Brown, A. L. (1984). Metacognition, executive control, self-regulation, and other even more mysterious mechanisms. In F. E. Weinert & R. H. Kluwe (Eds.), *Metacognition, motivation, and learning* (pp. 60–108). Stuttgart, West Germany: Kuhlhammer.

Brown, J. S., & Burton, R. R. (1978). Diagnostic models for procedural bugs in basic mathematical skills. *Cognitive Science, 2,* 155–192.

Bruner, J. (1960). *The process of education.* Cambridge, MA: Harvard University Press.

Buber, M. (1958). *I and thou.* New York: Scribner.

Caine, R. N., & Caine, G. (1991). *Making connections: Teaching and the human brain.* Alexandria, VA: Association for Supervision and Curriculum Development.

Calfee, R. C. (1994). *Implications for cognitive psychology for authentic assessment and instruction* (Tech. Rep. No. 69). Berkeley: University of California, National Center for the Study of Writing.

Calfee, R. C., & Hiebert, E. H. (1991). Classroom assessment of reading. In R. Barr, M. Kamil, P. Mosenthal, & P. D. Pearson (Eds.), *Handbook of research on reading* (2nd ed., pp. 281–309). New York: Longman.

Carnine, D. (1992). Introduction. In D. Carnine & E. J. Kameenui (Eds.), *Higher order thinking: Designing curriculum for mainstream students* (pp. 1–22). Austin, TX: Pro-ed.

Carnine, D., & Kameenui, E. J. (Eds.). (1992). *Higher order thinking: Designing curriculum for mainstream students.* Austin, TX: Pro-ed.

Carroll, J. B. (1964). Words, meanings, and concepts. *Harvard Educational Review, 34,* 178–202.

Carroll, J. B. (1993). *Human cognitive abilities: A survey of factor-analytic studies.* New York: Cambridge University Press.

Center for Civic Education. (1994). *National standards for civics and government.* Calabasas, CA: Author.

Chafe, W. L. (1970). *Meaning and structure of language.* Chicago: University of Chicago Press.

Clark, H. H., & Clark, E. V. (1977). *Psychology and language.* San Diego, CA: Harcourt Brace Jovanovich.

Clarke, J. H. (1991). Using visual organizers to focus on thinking. *Journal of Readers, 34*(7), 526–534.

Clement, J., Lockhead, J., & Mink, G. (1979). Translation difficulties in learning mathematics. *American Mathematical Monthly, 88,* 3–7.

College Entrance Examination Board. (1983). *Academic preparation for college: What students need to know and be able to do.* New York: Author.

Consortium of National Arts Education Associations. (1994). *National standards for arts education: What every young American should know and be able to do in the arts.* Reston, VA: Music Educators National Conference.

Cooper, C. R. (1983). Procedures for describing written texts. In P. Mosenthal, L. Tamor, & S. A. Walmsley (Eds.), *Research on writing* (pp. 287–313). New York: Longman.

Corno, L., Cronbach, L. J. (Ed.), Kupermintz, H., Lohman, D. F., Mandinach, E. B., Porteus, A.W., et al. for the Stanford Aptitude Seminar. (2002). *Remaking the concept of aptitude: Extending the legacy of Richard E. Snow.* Mahwah, NJ: Lawrence Erlbaum.

Costa, A. (1984). Mediating the metacognitive. *Educational Leadership, 42*(3), 57–62.

Costa, A. L. (1991). Toward a model of human intellectual functioning. In A. L. Costa (Ed.), *Developing minds: A resource book for teaching thinking* (Rev. ed., Vol. 1, pp. 137–140). Alexandria, VA: Association for Supervision and Curriculum Development.

Costa, A. L. (2001). *Developing minds: A resource book for teaching thinking* (3rd ed.). Alexandria, VA: Association for Supervision and Curriculum Development.

Costa, A. L., & Kallick, B. (2000). (Eds.). *Activating and engaging habits of mind.* Alexandria, VA: Association for Supervision and Curriculum Development.

Costa, A. L., & Kallick, B. (2004). *Assessment strategies for self-directed learning.* Thousand Oaks, CA: Corwin Press.

Covington, M. V. (1992). *Making the grade: A self-worth perspective on motivation and school reform.* New York: Cambridge University Press.

Csikszentmihalyi, M. (1990). *Flow: The psychology of optimal experience.* New York: Harper & Row.

Dale, E. (1967). Historical setting of programmed instruction. In P. C. Lange (Ed.), *Programmed instruction: Sixty-sixth yearbook of the National Society for the Study of Education, Part 2* (pp. 28–54). Chicago: University of Chicago Press.

Davis, R. B. (1984). *Learning mathematics: The cognitive science approach to mathematics education.* Norwood, NJ: Ablex.

de Beaugrande, R. (1980). *Text, discourse and process: Toward a multi-disciplinary science of text.* Norwood, NJ: Ablex.

Deely, J. (1982). *Semiotics: Its history and doctrine.* Bloomington: Indiana University Press.

de Kock, A., Sleegers, P., & Voeten, J. M. (2004). New learning and the classification of learning environments in secondary education. *Review of Educational Research, 74*(2), 141–170.

Dennett, D. C. (1969). *Content and consciousness.* London: Routledge & Kegan Paul.

Dennett, D. C. (1991). *Consciousness explained.* Boston: Little, Brown.

Dewey, J. (1916). *Democracy and education: An introduction to the philosophy of education.* New York: Macmillan.

Eco, U. (1976). *A theory of semiotics.* Bloomington: Indiana University Press.

Eco, U. (1979). *The role of the reader.* Bloomington: Indiana University Press.

Eco, U. (1984). *Semiotics and the philosophy of language.* Bloomington: Indiana University Press.

Education Commission of the States. (1982). *The information society: Are high school graduates ready?* Denver, CO: Education Commission of the States.

Education Testing Service. (1987). *Learning by doing: A manual for teaching and assessing higher order thinking in science and mathematics.* Princeton, NJ: Educational Testing Service.

Ehrenberg, S. D., Ehrenberg, L. M., & Durfee, D. (1979). *BASICS: Teaching/learning strategies.* Miami Beach, FL: Institute for Curriculum and Instruction.

Ennis, R. H. (1985). Goals for a critical thinking curriculum. In A. L. Costa (Ed.), *Developing minds: A resource book for teaching thinking* (pp. 54–57). Alexandria, VA: Association for Supervision and Curriculum Development.

Ennis, R. H. (1987a, Summer). A conception of critical thinking with some curriculum suggestions. *American Philosophical Association Newsletter on the Teaching of Philosophy,* 1–5.

Ennis, R. H. (1987b). A taxonomy of critical thinking dispositions and abilities. In J. Baron & R. Sternberg (Eds.), *Teaching thinking skills: Theory and practice* (pp. 9–26). New York: Freeman.

Ennis, R. H. (1989). Critical thinking and subject specificity: Clarification and needed research. *Educational Researcher, 18*(3), 4–10.

Ericsson, K. A., & Simon, H. A. (1980). Verbal reports as data. *Psychological Review, 87,* 215–251.

Ericsson, K. A., & Simon, H. A. (1984). *Protocol analysis: Verbal reports as data.* Cambridge: MIT Press.

Evans, J. St. B. T., Newstead, S. E., & Byrne, R. M. (1993). *Human reasoning.* Mahwah, NJ: Lawrence Erlbaum.

Fairbrother, R. W. (1975). The reliability of teachers' judgments of the ability being tested by multiple-choice items. *Educational Researcher, 17*(3), 202–210.

Fillmore, C. J. (1968). The case for case. In E. Beck & R. T. Harms (Eds.), *Universals in linguistic theory* (pp. 1–210). New York: Holt, Rinehart & Winston.

Fitts, P. M. (1964). Perceptual-motor skill learning. In A. W. Melton (Ed.), *Categories of human learning* (pp. 107–131). New York: John Wiley.

Flavell, J. (1979). Metacognition and cognitive monitoring: A new area of cognitive-developmental inquiry. *American Psychologist, 34,* 906–911.

Flavell, J. H. (1976). Metacognitive aspects of problem solving. In L. B. Resnick (Ed.), *The nature of intelligence* (pp. 231–235). Hillsdale, NJ: Lawrence Erlbaum.

Flavell, J. H. (1977). *Cognitive development.* Englewood Cliffs, NJ: Prentice Hall.

Flavell, J. H. (1978). Metacognitive development. In J. M. Scandura & C. J. Brainerd (Eds.), *Structural-process theories of complex human behavior* (pp. 213–245). Alpen a.d. Rijn, the Netherlands: Sijithoff and Noordhoff.

Flavell, J. H. (1987). Speculations about the nature and development of metacognition. In F. E. Weinert & R. H. Kluwe (Eds.), *Metacognition, motivation and understanding* (pp. 21–29). Hillsdale, NJ: Lawrence Erlbaum.

Frankl, V. E. (1967). *Psychotherapy and existentialism.* New York: Pocket Books.

Frederiksen, C. H. (1975). Representing logical and semantic structure of knowledge acquired from discourse. *Cognitive Psychology, 7,* 371–458.

Frederiksen, C. H. (1977). Semantic processing units in understanding text. In R. O. Freedle (Ed.), *Discourse production and comprehension* (Vol. 1, pp. 57–88). Norwood, NJ: Ablex.

Furst, E. J. (1994). Bloom's taxonomy: Philosophical and educational issues. In L. W. Anderson & L. A. Sosniak (Eds.), *Bloom's taxonomy: A forty-year retrospective: Ninety-third yearbook of the National Society for the Study of Education* (pp. 28–40). Chicago: University of Chicago Press.

Gagne, R. M. (1977). *The conditions of learning* (3rd ed.). New York: Holt, Rinehart & Winston.

Gagne, R. M. (1989). *Studies of learning: 50 years of research.* Tallahassee: Florida State University, Learning Systems Institute.

Garcia, T., & Pintrich, P. R. (1991, August). *The effects of autonomy on motivation, use of learning strategies, and performance in the college classroom.* Paper presented at the annual meeting of the American Psychological Association, San Francisco, CA.

Garcia, T., & Pintrich, P. R. (1993, August). *Self-schemas as goals and their role in self-regulated learning.* Paper presented at the annual meeting of the American Psychological Association, Toronto, Canada.

Garcia, T., & Pintrich, P. R. (1995, August). *The role of possible selves in adolescents' perceived competence and self-regulation.* Paper presented at the annual meeting of the American Educational Research Association, San Francisco, CA.

Gentner, D., & Markman, A. B. (1994). Structural alignment in comparison: No difference without similarity. *Psychological Science, 5*(3), 152–158.

Geography Education Standards Project. (1994). *Geography for life: National geography standards.* Washington, DC: National Geographic Research and Exploration.

Gilovich, T. (1991). *How we know what isn't so.* New York: Free Press.

Glaser, R. (1984). Education and thinking: The role of knowledge. *American Psychologist, 39,* 93–104.

Glaser, R. (1985). Learning and instructions: A letter for a time capsule. In S. F. Chipman, J. W. Segal, & R. Glaser (Eds.), *Thinking and learning skills: Research and open questions* (Vol. 2, pp. 609–618). Hillsdale, NJ: Lawrence Erlbaum.

Glaser, R., & Linn, R. (1993). Foreword. In L. Shepard, *Setting performance standards for student achievement* (pp. xiii–xiv). Stanford, CA: Stanford University, National Academy of Education.

Glasman, N. S., & Pellegrino, J. W. (Eds.). (1984). *Review of Educational Research* [Special issue], *54*(4).

Glasser, W. (1969). *Schools without failure.* New York: Harper & Row.

Glasser, W. (1981). *Stations of the mind.* New York: Harper & Row.

Goleman, D. (1995). *Emotional intelligence: Why it can matter more than IQ.* New York: Bantam.

Goodman, Y. M. (1978). Kid watching: An alternative to testing. *National Elementary School Principal, 57,* 41–45.

Halpern, D. F. (1984). *Thought and knowledge: An introduction to critical thinking.* Hillsdale, NJ: Lawrence Erlbaum.

Halpern, D. F. (1996a). *Thinking critically about critical thinking.* Mahwah, NJ: Lawrence Erlbaum.

Halpern, D. F. (1996b). *Thought & knowledge: An introduction to critical thinking* (3rd ed.). Mahwah, NJ: Lawrence Erlbaum.

Hart, L. A. (1983). *Human brain and human learning.* New York: Longman.

Harter, S. (1980). The perceived competence scale for children. *Child Development, 51,* 218–235.

Hayes, J. R. (1981). *The complete problem solver.* Philadelphia: Franklin Institute.

Heimlich, J. E., & Pittelman, S. D. (1988). *Semantic mapping: Classroom applications.* Newark, DE: International Reading Association.

Himsworth, H. (1986). *Scientific knowledge & philosophic thought.* Baltimore: Johns Hopkins University Press.

Hirsch, E. D., Jr. (1987). *Cultural literacy: What every American needs to know.* Boston: Houghton Mifflin.

Hirsch, E. D., Jr. (1996). *The schools we need: Why we don't have them.* New York: Doubleday.

Holland, J. H., Holyoak, K. F., Nisbett, R. E., & Thagard, P. R. (1986). *Induction: Processes of inference, learning, and discovery.* Cambridge: MIT Press.

Johnson-Laird, P. N. (1983). *Mental models.* Cambridge, MA: Harvard University Press.

Johnson-Laird, P. N. (1985). Logical thinking: Does it occur in daily life? In S. F. Chapman, J. W. Segal, & R. Glaser (Eds.), *Thinking and learning skills: Research and open questions* (Vol. 2, pp. 293–318). Hillsdale, NJ: Lawrence Erlbaum.

Johnson-Laird, P. N., & Byrne, R. M. J. (1991). *Deduction.* Hillsdale, NJ: Lawrence Erlbaum.

Joint Committee on National Health Education Standards. (1995). *National health education standards: Achieving health literacy.* Reston, VA: Association for the Advancement of Health Education.

Jones, B. F., Amiran, M., & Katims, M. (1985). Teaching cognitive strategies and text structures within language arts programs. In J. W. Segal, S. F. Chapman, & R. Glaser (Eds.), *Thinking and learning skills: Relating instruction to research* (Vol. 1, pp. 259–295). Hillsdale, NJ: Lawrence Erlbaum.

Jones, B. F., Palincsar, A. S., Ogle, D. S., & Carr, E. G. (1987). *Strategic teaching: Cognitive instruction in the content areas.* Alexandria, VA: Association for Supervision and Curriculum Development.

Kameenui, E. J. (1992). Toward a scientific pedagogy of learning disabilities. In D. Carnine & E. J. Kameenui (Eds.), *Higher order thinking: Designing curriculum for mainstream students* (pp. 247–267). Austin, TX: Pro-ed.

Katz, J. (1999). *How emotions work.* Chicago: University of Chicago Press.

Kendall, J. S. (2000). Topics: A roadmap to standards. *NASSP Bulletin, 84*(620), 37–48.

Kendall, J. S., & Marzano, R. J. (2005). *Content knowledge: A compendium of content standards for K–12 curriculum.* Aurora, CO: Mid-continent Research for Education and Learning.

Kendall, J. S., Ryan, S. E., & Richardson, A. T. (2005). *The systematic identification of performance standards.* Aurora, CO: Mid-continent Research for Education and Learning.

Kintsch, W. (1974). *The representation of meaning in memory.* Hillsdale, NJ: Lawrence Erlbaum.

Kintsch, W. (1979). On modeling comprehension. *Educational Psychologist, 1,* 3–14.

Klausner, S. Z. (1965). *The quest for self-control.* New York: Free Press.

Klausmeier, H. J. (1985). *Educational psychology* (5th ed.). New York: Harper & Row.

Klausmeier, H. J., & Sipple, T. (1980). *Learning and teaching concepts.* New York: Academic Press.

Kleinsasser, A. (1991, September). *Rethinking assessment: Who's the expert?* Paper presented at the Casper Outcomes Conference, Casper, WY.

Krathwohl, D. R., Bloom, B. J., & Masia, B. B. (1964). *Taxonomy of educational objectives: The classification of educational goals. Handbook II: Affective domain.* New York: McKay.

Krathwohl, D. R., & Payne, D. A. (1971). Defining and assessing educational objectives. In R. L. Thorndike (Ed.), *Educational measurement* (pp. 17–45). Washington, DC: American Council on Education.

Kreitzer, A. E., & Madaus, G. F. (1994). Empirical investigations of the hierarchial structure of the taxonomy. In L. W. Anderson & L. A. Sosniak (Eds.), *Bloom's taxonomy: A forty-year retrospective: Ninety-third yearbook of the National Society for the Study of Education* (pp. 64–81). Chicago: University of Chicago Press.

LaBerge, D. L. (1995). *Attentional processing: The brain's art of mindfulness.* Cambridge, MA: Harvard University Press.

LaBerge, D., & Samuels, S. J. (1974). Toward a theory of automatic information processing in reading. In H. Singer & R. B. Riddell (Eds.), *Theoretical models and processes of reading* (pp. 548–579). Newark, DE: International Reading Association.

Langer, E. J. (1989). *Mindfulness.* Reading, MA: Addison-Wesley.

Laufer, B., & Goldstein, Z. (2004). Testing vocabulary knowledge: Size, strength, and computer adaptiveness. *Language Learning, 54,* 469–523.

LeDoux, J. E. (1996). *The emotional brain: The mysterious underpinnings of emotional life.* New York: Simon & Schuster.

Lindsay, P. H., & Norman, D. A. (1977). *Human information processing.* New York: Academic Press.

Lindsley, O. R. (1972). From Skinner to precision teaching: The child knows best. In J. B. Jordan & L. S. Robbins (Eds.), *Let's try doing something else kind of thing* (pp. 1–11). Arlington, VA: Council on Exceptional Children.

Madaus, G. F., & Stufflebeam, D. (Eds.). (1989). *Educational evaluation: Classic works of Ralph W. Tyler.* Boston: Kluwer.

Mager, R. (1962). *Preparing instructional objectives.* Palo Alto, CA: Fearon.

Mandler, G. (1983). The nature of emotions. In J. Miller (Ed.), *States of mind* (pp. 136–153). New York: Pantheon.

Markman, A. B., & Gentner, D. (1993a). Splitting the differences: A structural alignment view of similarity. *Journal of Memory and Learning, 32,* 517–535.

Markman, A. B., & Gentner, D. (1993b). Structural alignment during similarity comparisons. *Cognitive Psychology, 25,* 431–467.

Markus, H., & Ruvulo, A. (1990). Possible selves: Personalized representations of goals. In L. Pervin (Ed.), *Goal concepts in psychology* (pp. 211–241). Hillsdale, NJ: Lawrence Erlbaum.

Marzano, R. J. (1992). *A different kind of classroom: Teaching with dimensions of learning.* Alexandria, VA: Association for Supervision and Curriculum Development.

Marzano, R. J. (1998). *A theory-based meta-analysis of research on instruction* (Technical Report). Aurora, CO: Mid-continent Regional Educational Laboratory.

Marzano, R. J. (2001). *Designing a new taxonomy of educational objectives.* Thousand Oaks, CA: Corwin Press.

Marzano, R. J. (2004). *Building background knowledge for academic achievement.* Alexandria, VA: Association for Supervision and Curriculum Development.

Marzano, R. J., Brandt, R. S., Hughes, C. S., Jones, B. F., Presseisen, B. Z., Rankin, S. C., et al. (1988). *Dimensions of thinking: A framework for curriculum and instruction.* Alexandria, VA: Association for Supervision and Curriculum Development.

Marzano, R. J., Gaddy, B. B., Foseid, M. C., Foseid, M. P., & Marzano, J. S. (2005). *A handbook for classroom management that works.* Alexandria, VA: Association for Supervision and Curriculum Development.

Marzano, R. J., & Kendall, J. S. (1996a). *A comprehensive guide to designing standards-based districts, schools, and classrooms.* Alexandria, VA: Association for Supervision and Curriculum Development.

Marzano, R. J., & Kendall, J. S. (1996b). *The fall and rise of standards-based education.* Alexandria, VA: National Association of State Boards of Education.

Marzano, R. J., Kendall, J. S., & Cicchinelli, L. F. (1998). *What Americans believe students should know: A survey of U.S. adults.* Aurora, CO: Mid-continent Regional Educational Laboratory.

Marzano, R. J., Kendall, J. S., & Gaddy, B. B. (1999). *Essential knowledge: The debate over what American students should know.* Aurora, CO: Mid-continent Regional Educational Laboratory.

Marzano, R. J., Paynter, D. E., & Doty, J. K. (2003). *The Pathfinder Project: Exploring the power of one: Teacher's manual.* Conifer, CO: Pathfinder.

Maslow, A. H. (1968). *Toward a psychology of being.* New York: Van Nostrand Reinhold.

Mathematical Science Education Board. (1990). *Reshaping school mathematics.* Washington, DC: National Academy Press.

Mayer, R. E. (1992). *Thinking, problem solving, and cognition* (2nd ed.). New York: Freeman.

McCombs, B. L. (1984). Processes and skills underlying intrinsic motivation to learn: Toward a definition of motivational skills training intervention. *Educational Psychologist, 19*, 197–218.

McCombs, B. L. (1986). The role of the self-system in self-regulated learning. *Contemporary Educational Psychology, 11*, 314–332.

McCombs, B. L., & Marzano, R. J. (1990). Putting the self in self-regulated learning: The self as agent in integrating will and skill. *Educational Psychologist, 25*(1), 51–69.

McCombs, B. L., & Pope, J. E. (1994). *Motivating hard to reach students.* Washington, DC: American Psychological Association.

McCombs, B. L., & Whisler, J. S. (1997). *The learner-centered classroom and school.* San Francisco: Jossey-Bass.

McTighe, J., & Lyman, F. T., Jr. (1988). Cueing thinking in the classroom: The promise of theory embedded tools. *Educational Leadership, 45*(7), 18–25.

Medawar, P. B. (1967). Two conceptions of science. In P. B. Medawar (Ed.), *The art of the soluble.* London: Methuen.

Medin, D., Goldstone, R. L., & Markman, A. B. (1995). Comparison and choice: Relations between similarity processes and decision processes. *Psychonomic Bulletin & Review, 2*(1), 1–19.

Meichenbaum, D., & Asarnow, J. (1979). Cognitive-behavioral modification and metacognitive development: Implications for the classroom. In P. C. Kendall & S. D. Hollon (Eds.), *Cognitive-behavioral interventions: Theory, research, and procedures* (pp. 11–35). New York: Academic.

Mervis, C. B. (1980). Category structure and the development of categorization. In R. J. Spiro, B. C. Bruce, & W. F. Brewer (Eds.), *Theoretical issues in reading comprehension* (pp. 279–307). Hillsdale, NJ: Lawrence Erlbaum.

Meyer, B. J. F. (1975). *The organization of prose and its effects on memory.* New York: American Elsevier.

Meyer, C. A. (1992). What's the difference between authentic and performance assessment? *Educational Leadership, 49*(8), 39–40.

Miller, G. A., Galanter, E., & Pribram, K. H. (1960). *Plans and the structure of behavior.* New York: Holt, Rinehart & Winston.

Moseley, D. (n.d.). *Thinking skills taxonomies for post-16 learners: An evaluation: Revised version of first progress report to LSDA.* Newcastle upon Tyne, UK: University of Newcastle upon Tyne, School of Education, Communication and Language Sciences.

Mullis, I. V. S., Owen, E. H., & Phillips, G. W. (1990). *America's challenge: Accelerating academic achievement (A summary of findings from 20 years of NAEP).* Princeton, NJ: Educational Testing Service.

Murphy, P. D. (1974). *Consumer education modules: A spiral process approach.* Washington, DC: Office of Education, North Dakota State University, Fargo, Curriculum Development in Vocational and Technical Education.

Nardi, A. H., & Wales, C. E. (1985). Teaching decision-making: What to teach and how to teach it. In A. L. Costa (Ed.), *Developing minds: A resource book for teaching thinking* (pp. 220–223). Alexandria, VA: Association for Supervision and Curriculum Development.

National Association for Sport and Physical Education. (2004). *Moving into the future: National standards for physical education* (2nd ed.). Reston, VA: Author.

National Center for History in the Schools. (1994a). *National standards for history for grades K–4: Expanding children's world in time and space.* Los Angeles: Author.

National Center for History in the Schools. (1994b). *National standards for United States history: Exploring the American experience.* Los Angeles: Author.

National Center for History in the Schools. (1994c). *National standards for world history: Exploring paths to the present.* Los Angeles: Author.

National Center for History in the Schools. (1996). *National standards for history: Basic edition.* Los Angeles: Author.

National Commission on Excellence in Education. (1983). *A nation at risk: The imperative for educational reform.* Washington, DC: Government Printing Office.

National Council for the Social Studies. (1994). *Expectations of excellence: Curriculum standards for social studies.* Washington, DC: Author.

National Council of Teachers of English and the International Reading Association. (1996). *Standards for the English language arts.* Urbana, IL: National Council of Teachers of English.

National Council of Teachers of Mathematics. (2000). *Principles and standards for school mathematics.* Reston, VA: Author.

National Council on Economic Education. (1996, August). *Content statements for state standards in economics K–12.* Unpublished manuscript. New York: Author.

National Education Goals Panel. (1991). *The national education goals report: Building a nation of learners.* Washington, DC: Author.

National Research Council. (1996). *National science education standards.* Washington, DC: National Academy Press.

National Standards in Foreign Language Education Project. (1999). *Standards for foreign language learning in the 21st century.* Lawrence, KS: Author.

Newmann, F. M., Secado, W. G., & Wehlage, G. G. (1995). *A guide to authentic instruction and assessment: Vision, standards and scoring.* Madison: University of Wisconsin, Wisconsin Center for Educational Research.

Nickerson, R. S., Perkins, D. N., & Smith, E. E. (1985). *The teaching of thinking.* Hillsdale, NJ: Lawrence Erlbaum.

Norman, D. A., & Rumelhart, D. E. (1975). *Explanations in cognition.* New York: Freeman.

Paivio, A. (1969). Mental imagery in associative learning and memory. *Psychological Review, 76,* 241–263.

Paivio, A. (1971). *Imagery and verbal processing.* New York: Holt, Rinehart & Winston.

Paris, S. G., Lipson, M. Y., & Wixson, K. K. (1983). Becoming a strategic reader. *Contemporary Educational Psychology, 8*(3), 293–316.

Paul, R. (1990). *Critical thinking: What every person needs to survive in a rapidly changing world.* Rohnert Park, CA: Center for Critical Thinking and Moral Critique, Sonoma State University.

Paul, R. W. (1984). Critical thinking: Fundamental to education for a free society. *Educational Leadership, 42*(1), 4–14.

Paul, R. W. (1986a, December). *Critical thinking, moral integrity, and citizenship: Teaching for the intellectual virtues.* Paper distributed at ASCD Wingspread Conference on Teaching Skills, Racine, WI.

Percy, W. (1975). *The message in the bottle.* New York: Farrar, Strauss & Giroux.

Perkins, D. N. (1984). Creativity by design. *Educational Leadership, 42*(1), 18–25.

Perkins, D. N. (1985). *Where is creativity?* Paper presented at University of Iowa Second Annual Humanities Symposium, Iowa City, IA.

Perkins, D. N. (1986). *Knowledge as design.* Hillsdale, NJ: Lawrence Erlbaum.

Perkins, D. N., Allen, R., & Hafner, J. (1983). Difficulties in everyday reasoning. In W. Maxwell (Ed.), *Thinking: The expanding frontier* (pp. 177–189). Philadelphia: Franklin Institute Press.

Pert, C. B. (1997). *Molecules of emotion: Why you feel the way you feel.* New York: Scribner.

Piaget, J. (1971). *Genetic epistemology* (E. Duckworth, Trans.). New York: Norton.

Pintrich, P. R., & Garcia, T. C. (1992, April). *An integrated model of motivation and self-regulated learning.* Paper presented at the annual meeting of the American Educational Research Association, San Francisco, CA.

Poole, R. L. (1972). Characteristics of the taxonomy of educational objectives, cognitive domain: A replication. *Psychology in the Schools, 9*(1), 83–88.

Project 2061, American Association for the Advancement of Science. (1993). *Benchmarks for science literacy.* New York: Oxford University Press.

Reeves, D. B. (2002). *Holistic accountability: Serving students, schools, and community.* Thousand Oaks, CA: Corwin Press.

Resnick, L. (1987). *Education and learning to think.* Washington, DC: National Academy Press.

Richardson, A. (1983). Imagery: Definitions and types. In A. A. Sheikh (Ed.), *Imagery: Current theory, research, and application* (pp. 3–42). New York: John Wiley.

Rohwer, W. D., & Sloane, K. (1994). Psychological perspectives. In L. W. Anderson & L. A. Sosniak (Eds.), *Bloom's taxonomy: A forty-year retrospective: Ninety-third yearbook of the National Society for the Study of Education* (pp. 41–63). Chicago: University of Chicago Press.

Romberg, T. A., & Carpenter, T. P. (1986). Research on teaching and learning mathematics: Two disciplines of scientific inquiry. In M. C. Wittrock (Ed.), *Handbook of research on teaching* (3rd ed., pp. 850–873). New York: Macmillan.

Ross, J. A. (1988). Controlling variables: A meta-analysis of training studies. *Review of Educational Research, 58*(4), 405–437.

Ross, J., & Lawrence, K. A. (1968). Some observation on memory artifice. *Psychonomic Science, 13,* 107–108.

Rowe, H. (1985). *Problem solving and intelligence.* Hillsdale, NJ: Lawrence Erlbaum.

Rumelhart, D. E., & Norman, D. A. (1981). Accretion, tuning and restructuring: Three modes of learning. In J. W. Colton & R. Klatzky (Eds.), *Semantic factors in cognition* (pp. 37–53). Hillsdale, NJ: Lawrence Erlbaum.

Salomon, G., & Globerson, T. (1987). Skill may not be enough: The role of mindfulness in learning and transfer. *International Journal of Educational Research, 11,* 623–637.

Schank, R. C., & Abelson, R. (1977). *Scripts, plans, goals and understanding.* Hillsdale, NJ: Lawrence Erlbaum.

Seligman, M. E. P. (1990). *Learned optimism.* New York: Pocket Books.

Seligman, M. E. P. (1994). *What you can change and what you can't.* New York: Knopf.

Shepard, L. (1993). *Setting performance standards for student achievement: A report of the National Academy of Education Panel on the evaluation of the*

NAEP trial state assessment: An evaluation of the 1992 achievement levels. Stanford, CA: Stanford University, National Academy of Education.

Smith, E. E., & Medin, D. L. (1981). *Categories and concepts.* Cambridge, MA: Harvard University Press.

Snow, R. E., & Lohman, D. F. (1989). Implications of cognitive psychology for educational measurement. In R. L. Linn (Ed.), *Educational measurement* (3rd ed., pp. 263–331). New York: American Council on Education, & Macmillan.

Snowman, J., & McCown, R. (1984, April). *Cognitive processes in learning: A model for investigating strategies and tactics.* Paper presented at the annual meeting of the American Educational Research Association, New Orleans, LA.

Spearman, C. (1927). *The abilities of man: Their nature and measurement.* New York: Macmillan.

Stahl, R. J. (1985). *Cognitive information processes and processing within a uniprocess and processing within a uniprocess superstructure/microstructure framework: A practical information-based model.* Unpublished manuscript, University of Arizona, Tucson.

Stanley, J. C., & Bolton, D. (1957). A review of Bloom's taxonomy of educational objectives and J. R. Gerberich's specimen objective test items: A guide to achievement test construction. *Educational and Psychological Measurement, 17*(4), 631–634.

Sternberg, R. J. (1977). *Intelligence, information processing and analogical reasoning: The componential analysis of human abilities.* Hillsdale, NJ: Lawrence Erlbaum.

Sternberg, R. J. (1984a). *Beyond IQ: A triarchic theory of human intelligence.* New York: Cambridge University Press.

Sternberg, R. J. (1984b). Mechanisms of cognitive development: A componential approach. In R. J. Sternberg (Ed.), *Mechanisms of cognitive development* (pp. 163–186). New York: Freeman.

Sternberg, R. J. (1986a). Inside intelligence. *American Scientist, 74,* 137–143.

Sternberg, R. J. (1986b). *Intelligence applied.* New York: Harcourt Brace Jovanovich.

Sternberg, R. J. (1987). Most vocabulary is learned from context. In M. G. McKeown & M. E. Curtis (Eds.), *The nature of vocabulary acquisition* (pp. 89–105). Hillsdale, NJ: Lawrence Erlbaum.

Sternberg, R. J., & Spear-Swerling, L. (1996). *Teaching for thinking.* Washington, DC: American Psychological Association.

Stiggins, R. J. (1994). *Student-centered classroom assessment.* New York: Merrill.

Taba, H. (1967). *Teacher's handbook for elementary social studies.* Reading, MA: Addison-Wesley.

Tennyson, R. D., & Cocchiarella, M. J. (1986). An empirically based instructional design theory for teaching concepts. *Review of Educational Research, 56,* 40–71.

Tilton, J.W. (1926). *The relationship between association and higher mental processes: Teachers College contributions to education, No. 218.* New York: Bureau of Publications, Teachers College.

Toulmin, S., Rieke, R., & Janik, A. (1981). *An introduction to reasoning.* New York: Macmillan.

Travers, R. M. W. (1950). *How to make achievement tests.* New York: Odyssey.

Turner, A., & Greene, E. (1977). *The construction of a propositional text base.* Boulder: The University of Colorado, Institute for the Study of Intellectual Behavior.

Tweney, R. D., Doherty, M. E., & Mynatt, C. R. (1981). *On scientific thinking.* New York: Columbia University Press.

Tyler, R. W. (1949a). *Basic principles of curriculum and instruction.* Chicago: University of Chicago Press.

Tyler, R. W. (1949b). *Constructing achievement tests.* Chicago: University of Chicago Press.

van Dijk, T. A. (1977). *Text and context.* London: Longman.

van Dijk, T. A. (1980). *Macrostructures.* Hillsdale, NJ: Lawrence Erlbaum.

van Dijk, T. A., & Kintsch, W. (1983). *Strategies of discourse comprehension.* Hillsdale, NJ: Lawrence Erlbaum.

van Eemeren, F. H., Grootendorst, R., & Henkemans, F. S. (1996). *Fundamentals of argumentation theory: A handbook of historical backgrounds and contemporary developments.* Mahwah, NJ: Lawrence Erlbaum.

Wahba, N. A., & Bridwell, L. G. (1976). Maslow reconsidered: A review of research on the need of hierarchy theory. *Organizational Behavior and Human Performance, 15,* 212–240.

Wales, C. E., Nardi, A. H., & Stager, R. A. (1986). Decision making: New paradigm for education. *Educational Leadership, 43*(8), 37–41.

Wales, C. E., & Stager, R. A. (1977). *Guided design.* Morgantown: West Virginia University Center for Guided Design.

Wang, M. C., Haertel, G. D., & Walberg, H. J. (1993). Toward a knowledge base for school learning. *Review of Educational Research, 63*(3), 249–294.

Waples, D., & Tyler, R.W. (1934). *Research methods and teachers' problems: A manual for systematic study of classroom procedures.* New York: Macmillan.

Wickelgren, W. A. (1974). *How to solve problems.* San Francisco: Walt Freeman.

Wiggins, G., & McTighe, J. (1998). *Understanding by design.* Alexandria, VA: Association for Supervision and Curriculum Development.

Wilde, S. (Ed.). (1996). *Notes from a kid watcher: Selected writings of Yetta M. Goodman.* Portsmouth, NH: Heinemann.

Wood, B. N. (1923). *Measurement in higher education.* Yonkers-on-Hudson, NY: World Book.

Zimmerman, B. J., Bonner, S., & Kovach, R. (1996). *Developing self-regulated learners.* Washington, DC: American Psychological Association.

Index

CORWIN PRESS

The Corwin Press logo—a raven striding across an open book—represents the union of courage and learning. Corwin Press is committed to improving education for all learners by publishing books and other professional development resources for those serving the field of PreK–12 education. By providing practical, hands-on materials, Corwin Press continues to carry out the promise of its motto: **"Helping Educators Do Their Work Better."**